Artistic Transmissions:

The Art and Lore of

Galaxy Prime
A Sci-Fi Roleplaying Epic

by

James Shade

Original Art

Amy Fanning

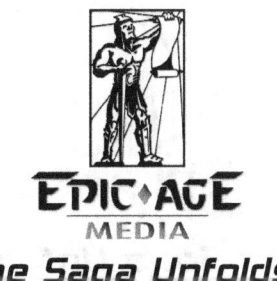

EPIC AGE
MEDIA
"The Saga Unfolds..."

Artistic Transmissions:
The Art and Lore of
GALAXY PRIME

by

James Shade

Original Art

Amy Fanning

Printed with pride in the United States of America

Revised Edition 2015

www.EpicAgeMedia.com

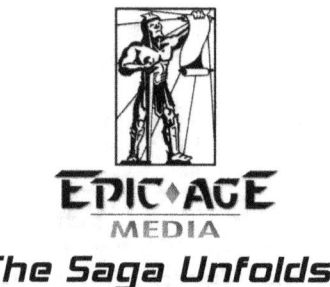

EPIC AGE
MEDIA

"The Saga Unfolds..."

Foreword

Incoming Transmission!

Big, bold and beautiful! These visual depictions of species from another galaxy are absolutely phenomenal! See how the lines delineate their every detail? See how their expressions speak volumes? Truly uncanny is their similarity to our own lifeforms! But the variations are myriad! It strikes me as amazing that so many sentient beings could evolve in so many different forms and fashions in such a distant place that is apparently not unlike our own. The artist has masterfully captured their attitudes and emotions. Their postures and manner of dress are indicative of their lifestyles, be it peaceful or violent, creative or technical. What a wonder to theorize on how these races interact with each other and the world around them. Some seem so primitive and yet they are capable of handling the concepts of space travel and quantum physics! Given the small sampling of examples here, I have no doubt that there are many, many more types of creatures great and small, sentient and otherwise inhabiting this far away place called Galaxy Prime...

Arn Blademaster

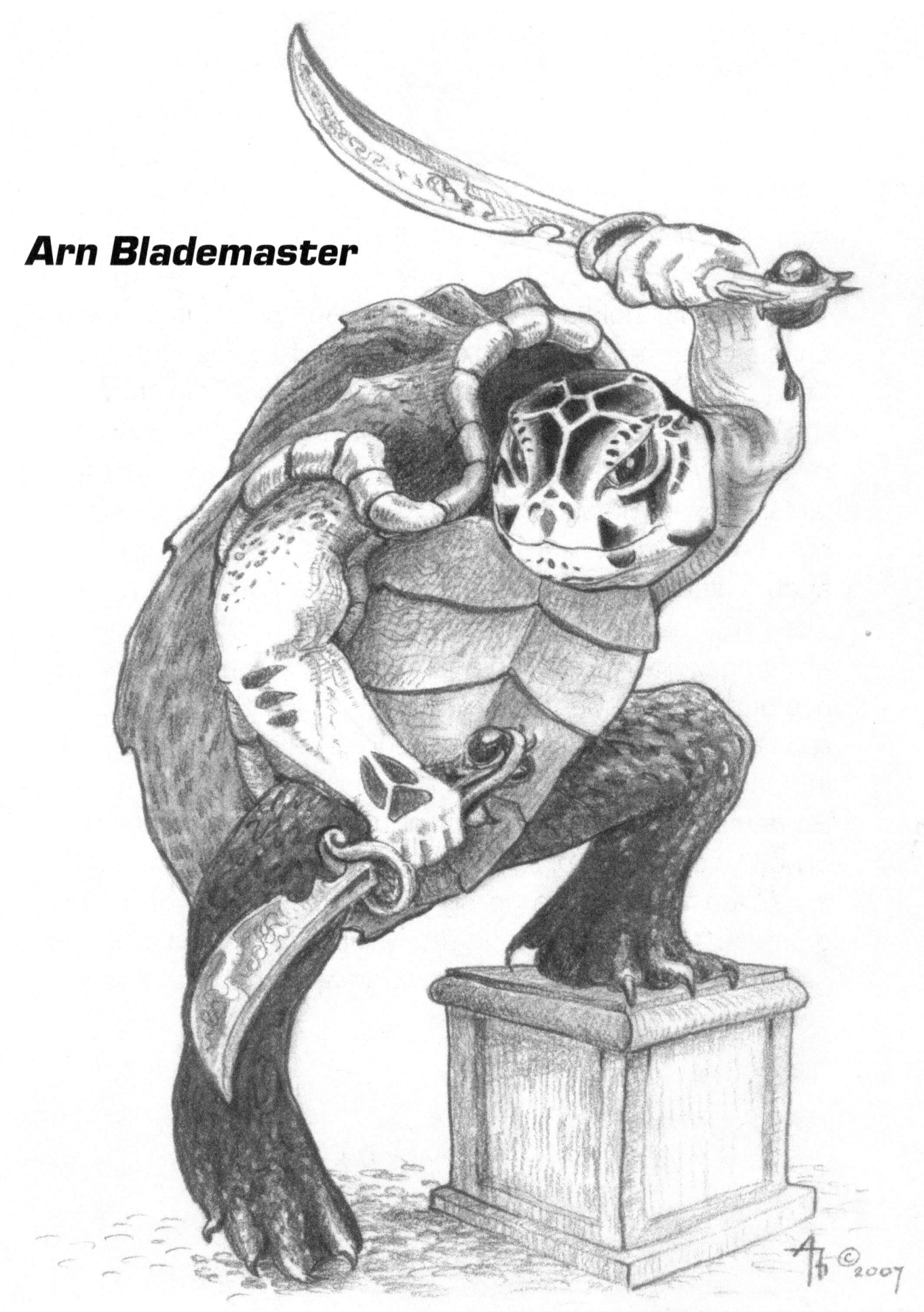

Species Report - Arn
Home Sector - Arn Sovereignty
Homeworld - Arn (Coordinates 14.8.12)
Planets in System - 3
Habitable Planets - 1
Planets Inhabited - 1
Planetary Gravity - 3 (Standard)
Dominant Climate - Desert
Technological Level - 4 (Spacefaring)
Governmental Structure - Theocracy (Leader: High Theologian)
Societal Norm - Piousness
Cultural Emphasis - Wisdom, Honor
Miscellaneous Traits - Brave, Altruistic
Lifespan - 400 years
Physical Attributes - 1.8m height; 175 pounds; full-body carapace (removable); deep yellow/brown skin tones; red eyes; entire body can be compressed to fit within carapace; vegetarian diet; mated reproduction with eggs laid (4-6) and buried in sandy pits

Summary - A benevolent, non-amphibious race. The first in their sector to achieve space travel. A complex polytheistic religious system involving pilgrimages to the Khuri nebula, believed to be the sacred domain of their pantheon. Very protective of this locale, allowing no entry. Likewise, the Cherun nebula is viewed as a sort of underworld and travelers are discouraged from visiting it. No interest in colonization of other worlds but take every opportunity to spread their holy doctrine, even revising and adapting it to suit the needs of others.

     Critical disputes are settled using ceremonial duelling blades, though these rarely end in fatality. Shell prevents a good deal of physical damage but is often discarded by those entering the clergy, allegedly relying on their faith to protect them. On good terms with the Liyek, Ziryan, Vorhusk and Molgans. Allies of the Sulven League. Affirmed enemies of the Runarians and the Tuth.

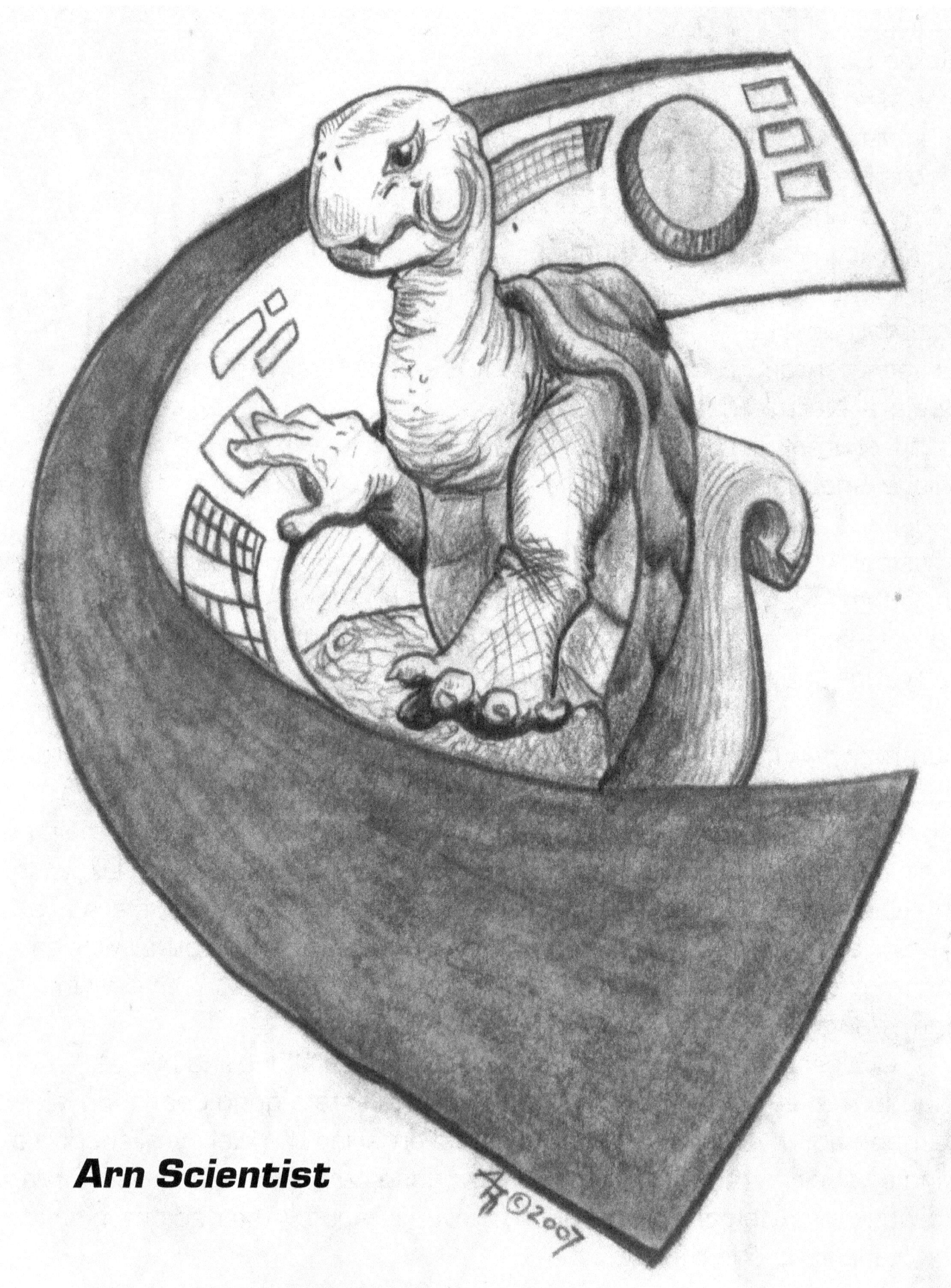

Arn Scientist

Their vessels (often configured to resemble their own shells) can traverse land, sea, air and space, though they make efforts to avoid aquatic travel whenever possible. Preference is for defense using non-lethal weaponry. Excellent melee combatants despite their apparent lack of dexterity.

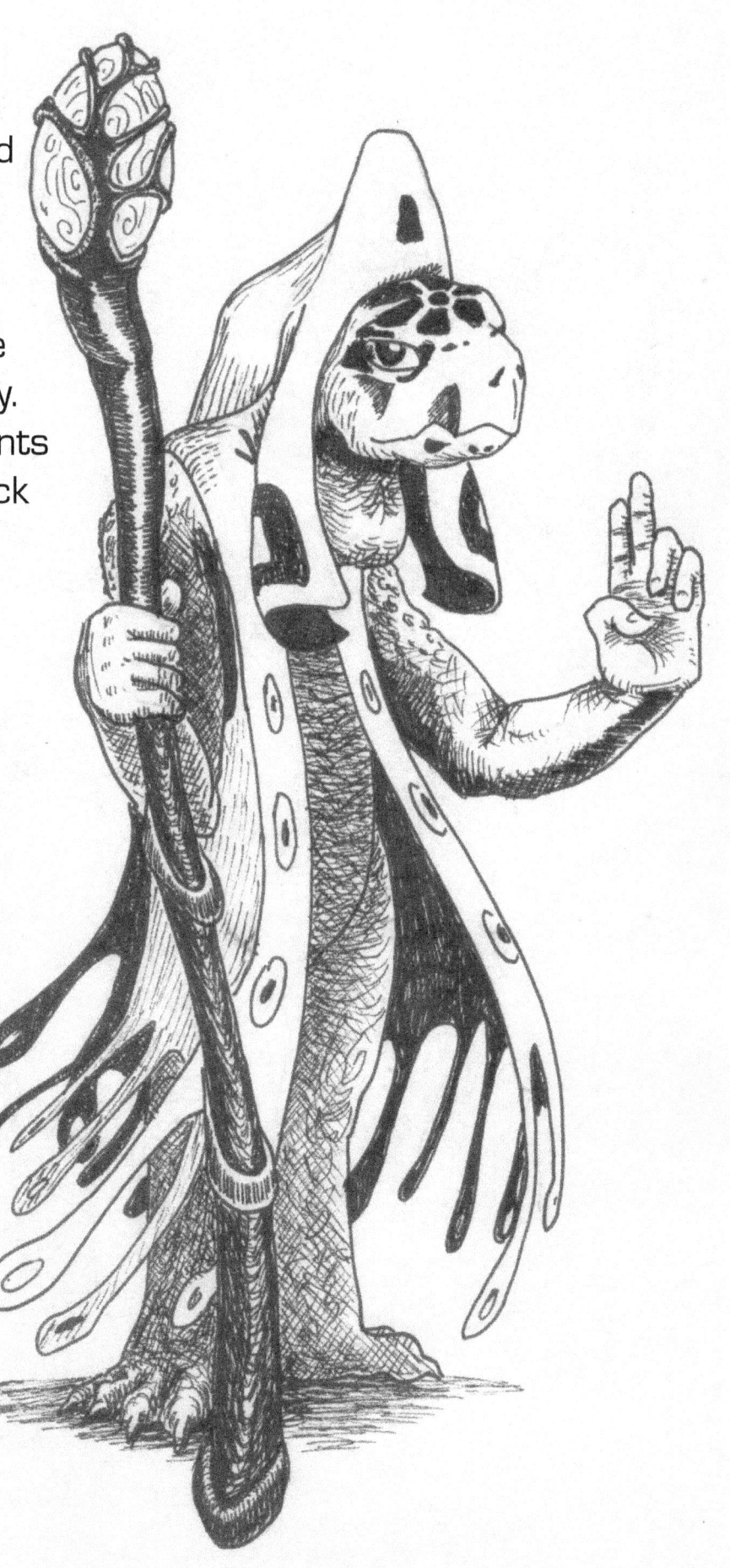

Arn Cleric

**Buthari
Brawler**

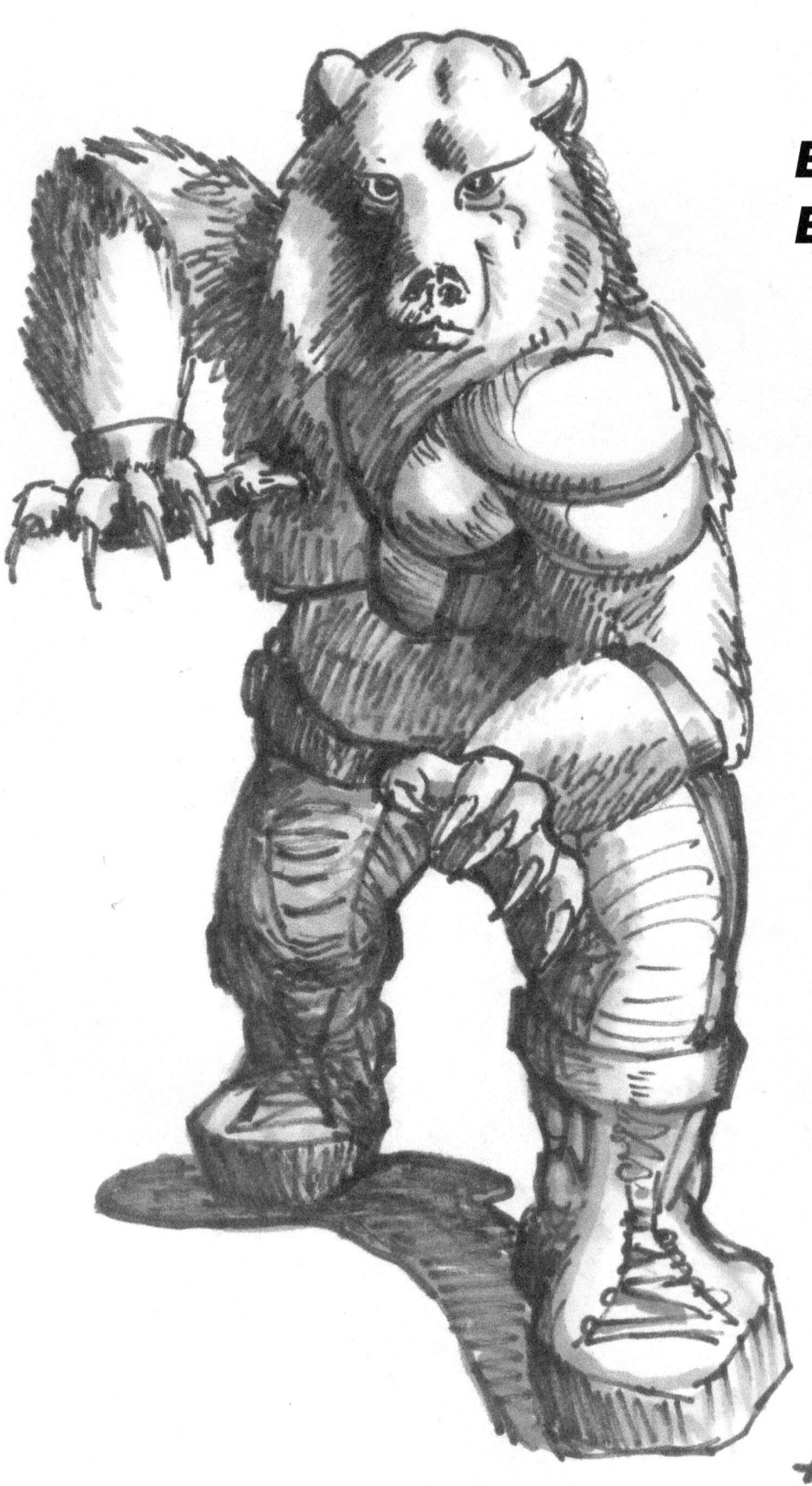

Expanded Buthari Timeline

5C - Primitive Buthari live in caves or as nomads

1M1C - Visited by Sovaari

1M2C - Earliest cities and governments formed

1M8C - Buthari civil war

2M3C - Global disaster; Buthari nearly extinct; saved only by hibernating

2M5C - Society rebuilt

2M9C - First Buthari Kinet discovered

3M3C - Grengi traders arrive

3M6C - Industrial revolution

4M1C - Runarians invade; claim land and resources

4M5C - Kunlaati harass Buthada; Runarians and Buthari band together/share knowledge

4M8C - Joint space program initiated

5M2C - Second planet in Buthada system colonized

5M4C - Third planet in Buthada system colonized

5M7C - Runarians tighten grip in response to Drakasian rebellion

6M3C - Nommes explore Buthada and befriend Buthari; friction between Runarians heightens

6M5C - Buthari begin passive resistance against Runarian rule

6M9C - Plague weakens Runarian garrison

7M2C - Buthari wander galaxy seeking allies and other worlds to colonize

7M6C - Buthari openly rebel against Runarians; homeworld blockaded

8M1C - Buthari make deals with Tuth crime cartels to undermine Runarians

8M3C - Arn delegation arrives to negotiate peace; is never heard from again

8M7C - Runarian Monarchy officially condemned by gathering of galactic leaders; sanctions imposed

9M3C - Lkri strike forces inflict massive damage on Runarian blockade

9M5C - In wake of Drakasian emancipation, Runarians re-deploy and strengthen Buthada blockade

10M2C - Kinet arrive and collect their Buthari brethren

10M6C - Mordas prophecy leads to increased pressure on Runarians and desperation in Buthari

10M9C - Sulven and Vorhusk researchers smuggle Buthari off-planet

11M - Buthari refugees join the Advocates for Galactic Council and assist with Provion Project

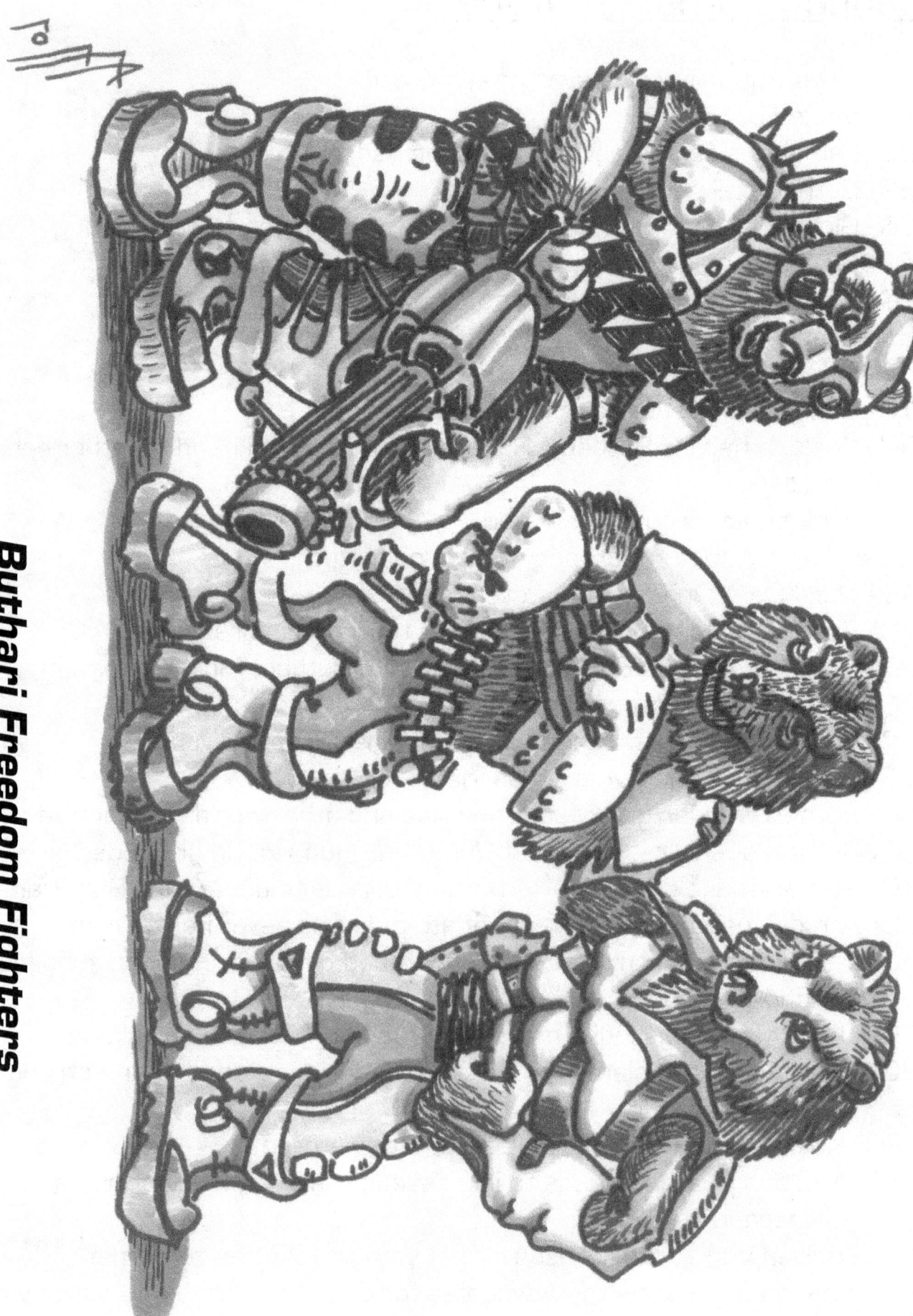

Buthari Freedom Fighters

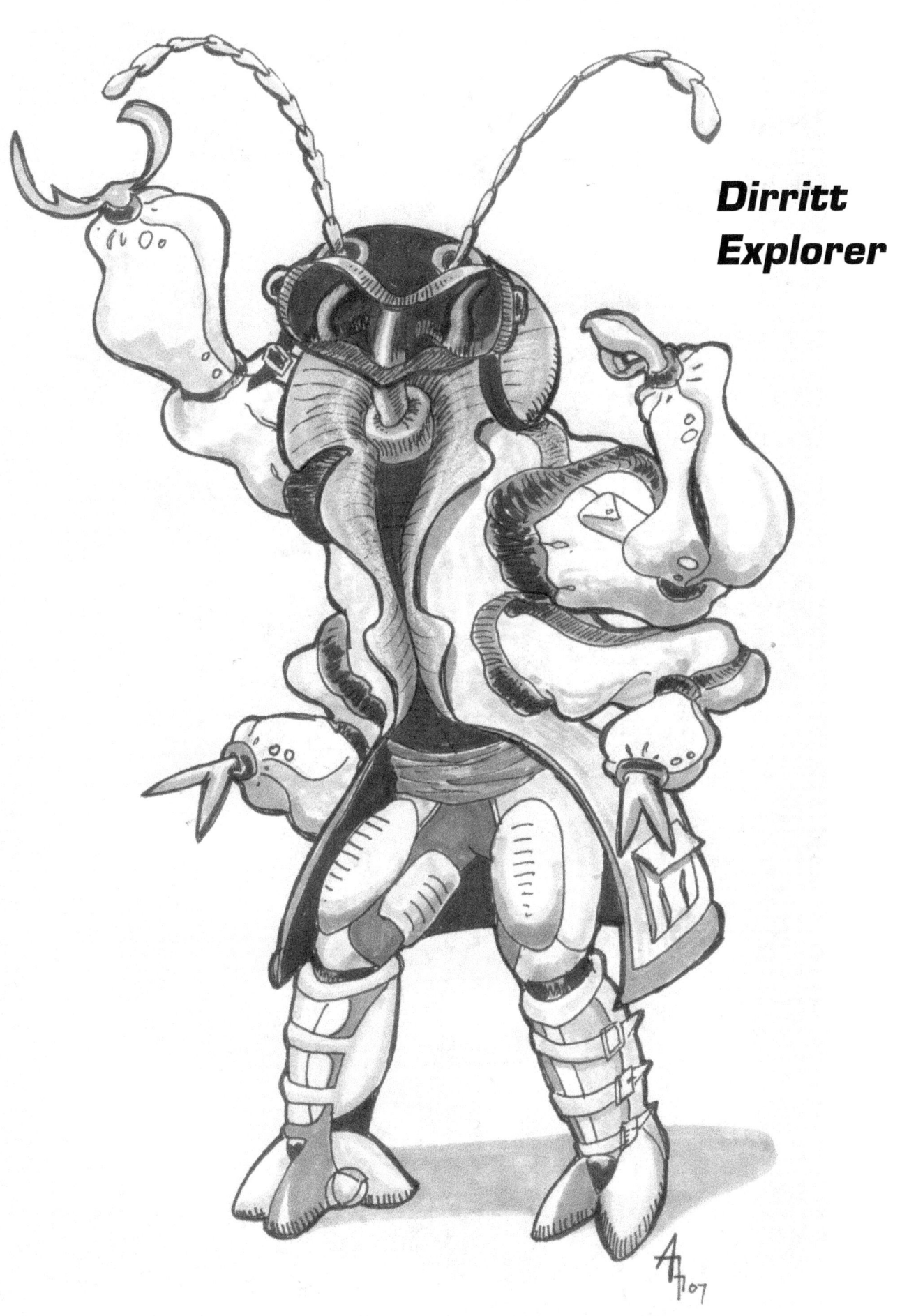

Dirritt Explorer

**Dirritt
Assassin**

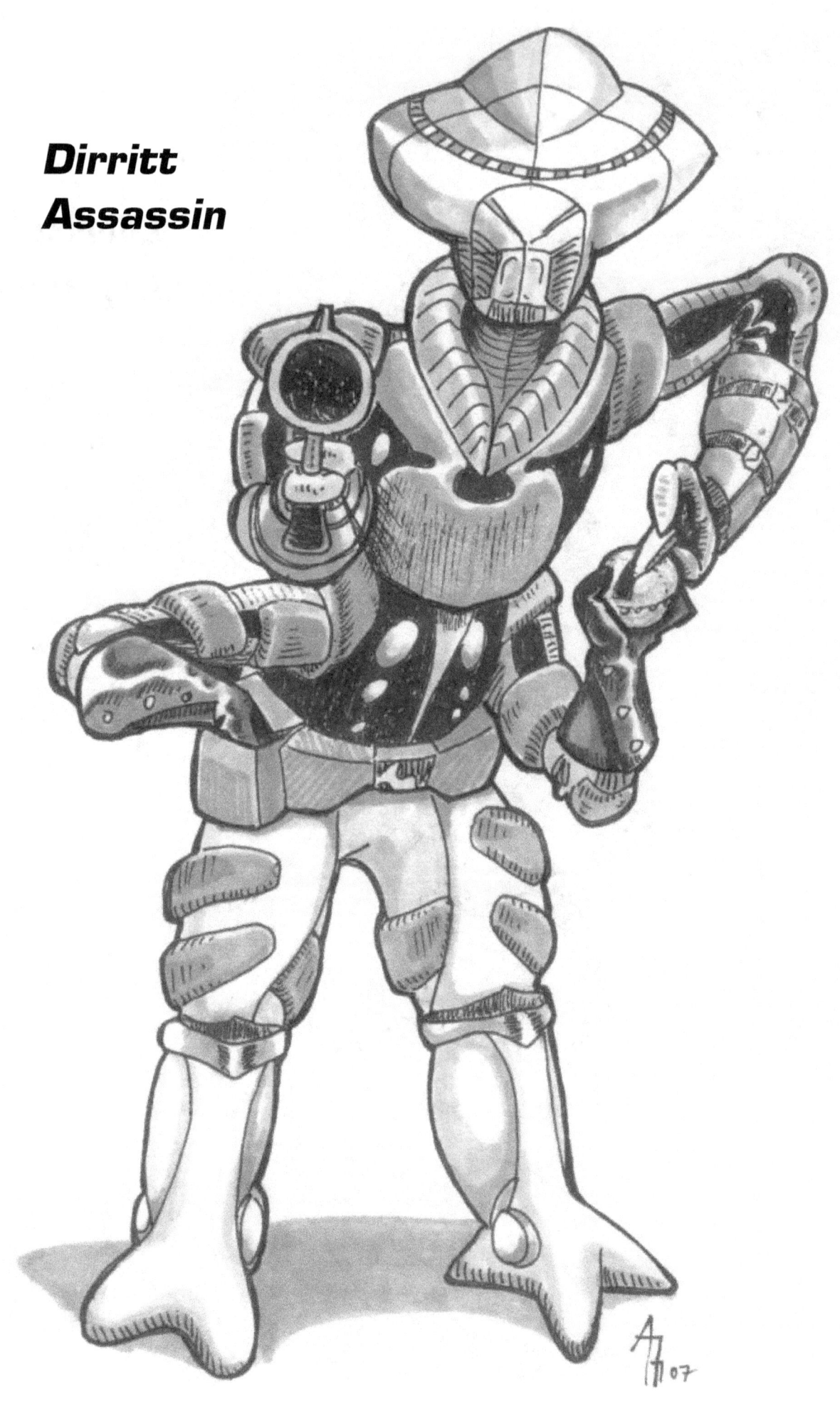

Wanted Poster

NAME - Ijnix
SPECIES - Dirritt

STRENGTH - 15
INTELLIGENCE - 21
DEXTERITY - 16
SPEED - 48
PRPJECTILE WEAPONS - 67
HAND TO HAND - 61
DEFENSE - 53
OBSERVATION - 73
WILLFORCE - 56
LUCK - 52

SKILLS - Medical, Xenoscience, Robotics
CRIMES - Kidnapping, Torture, Murder, Theft
BOUNTY - 200,000; Alive; THASIAN AUTOCRACY, TRIUMVIRATE SPACE
LAST SEEN - Free Space

DATA - Ijnix was convinced that she could find a way to integrate cyberware into the bodies of her people, the Dirritt being one of the few races in Galaxy Prime that was unable to utilize the high tech artificial upgrades. She started by experimenting on the corpses of Dirritt criminals. When those results were inconclusive she moved on to live subjects. Needing more cyberware to modify and tinker with, she stole great shipments from the Exomechs, as well as kidnapping some of their leading scientists, hoping to glean information from their vast experience with the materials. She would say that she is only trying to improve the lot of her people and bring them on to the galactic stage in a manner befitting their alleged status as a "race of import".

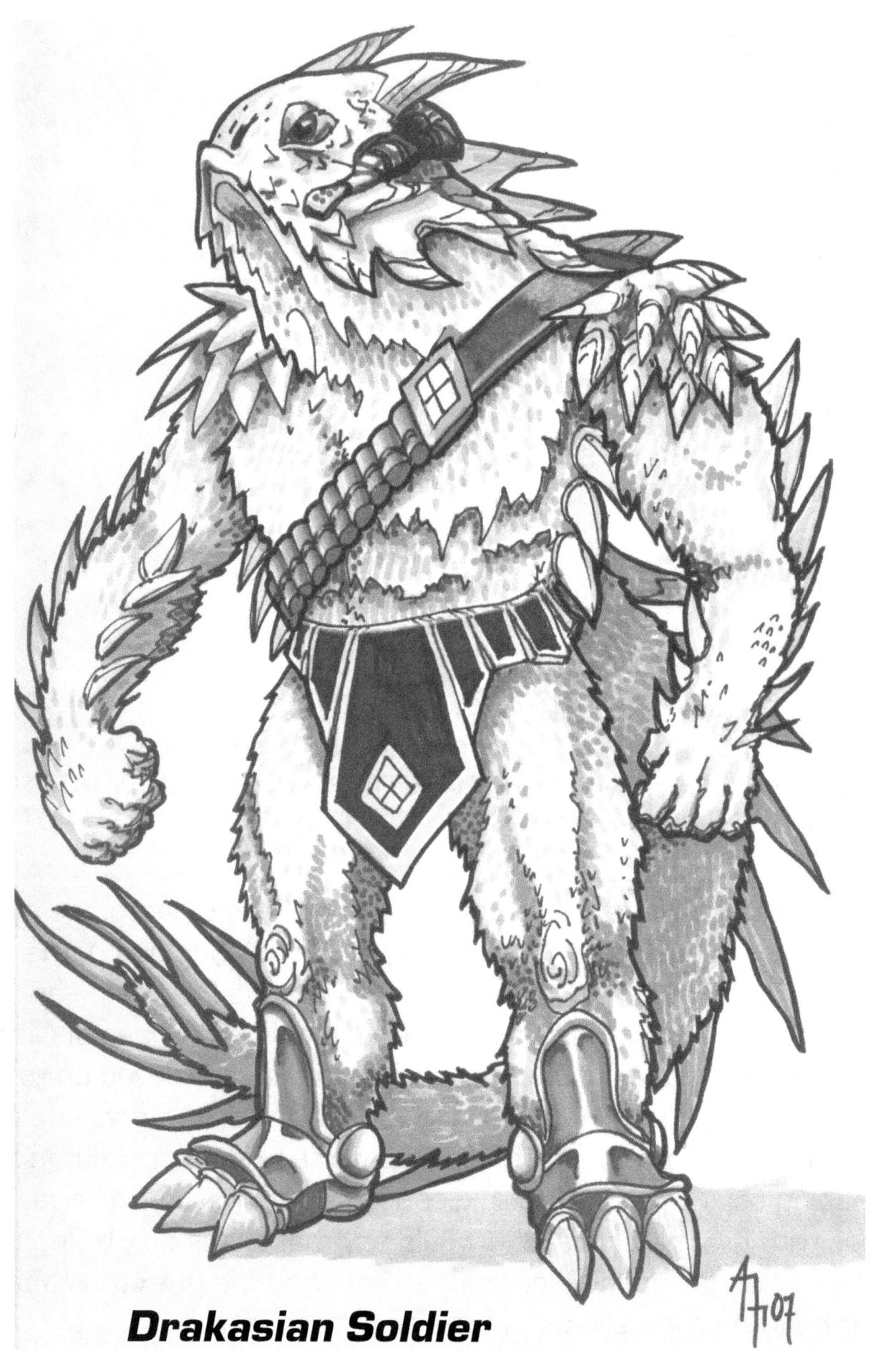

Drakasian Soldier

Drakasian Journal

An abridged version of the journal written by World Leader Eshrex with excerpts highlighting some of the major events in his long and distinguished career.

Age 19 - Rode a vash for the first time. Hard to subdue. Had to ambush. An excellent mount. I have a talent for riding. Parent suggested I join the Drak scouts. More training ahead.

Age 27 - First mission to Sinde belt. Met with Liyekan smugglers. Acquired weapons and equipment for Drak resistance. Smooth transaction.

Age 33 - Help strike crushing blow to Runarians at Battle of Stel-17. Victory decisive. Runarians fall back to home sector. Promoted to Kill Leader.

Age 38 - Negotiate non-aggression pact with Thasians. Subsequent trade pact supplies much needed materiel for reconstruction effort. Promoted to Over Leader.

Age 41 - Met with Dolg of Tuth crime cartel. Accepted his offer of payment in exchange for non-interference with his base on Gelra and operations throughout the sector.

Age 45 - Signs of rebellion from Kywokks, Vosskans and Muots. My strike force rushes to quell these insurrections. Attacks are successful but situation remains unstable. Promoted to Grand Leader.

Age 52 - Used wormhole WH-C2 to visit Kor Regime. A strong people with similar ideals. Agreed to small Kor garrison in Drakasian Annex to assist with civil unrest. Possible alliance in the works.

Age 60 - Charged with hunting down the rogue assassin Ravitha. His actions continue to kill many Runarians but endanger the Kor alliance.

Age 67 - Form pacts with many of the Free Colonies. Tuth are outraged but Runarians are fearful. Promoted to Sector Leader.

Age 74 - World Leader Shrevvex dies in office. I assume command of our people and claim his title.

(World Leader Eshrex was killed in an explosion while visiting the second moon of Drak as the result of a Runarian plot to throw the sector into anarchy. He was aged 83 years.)

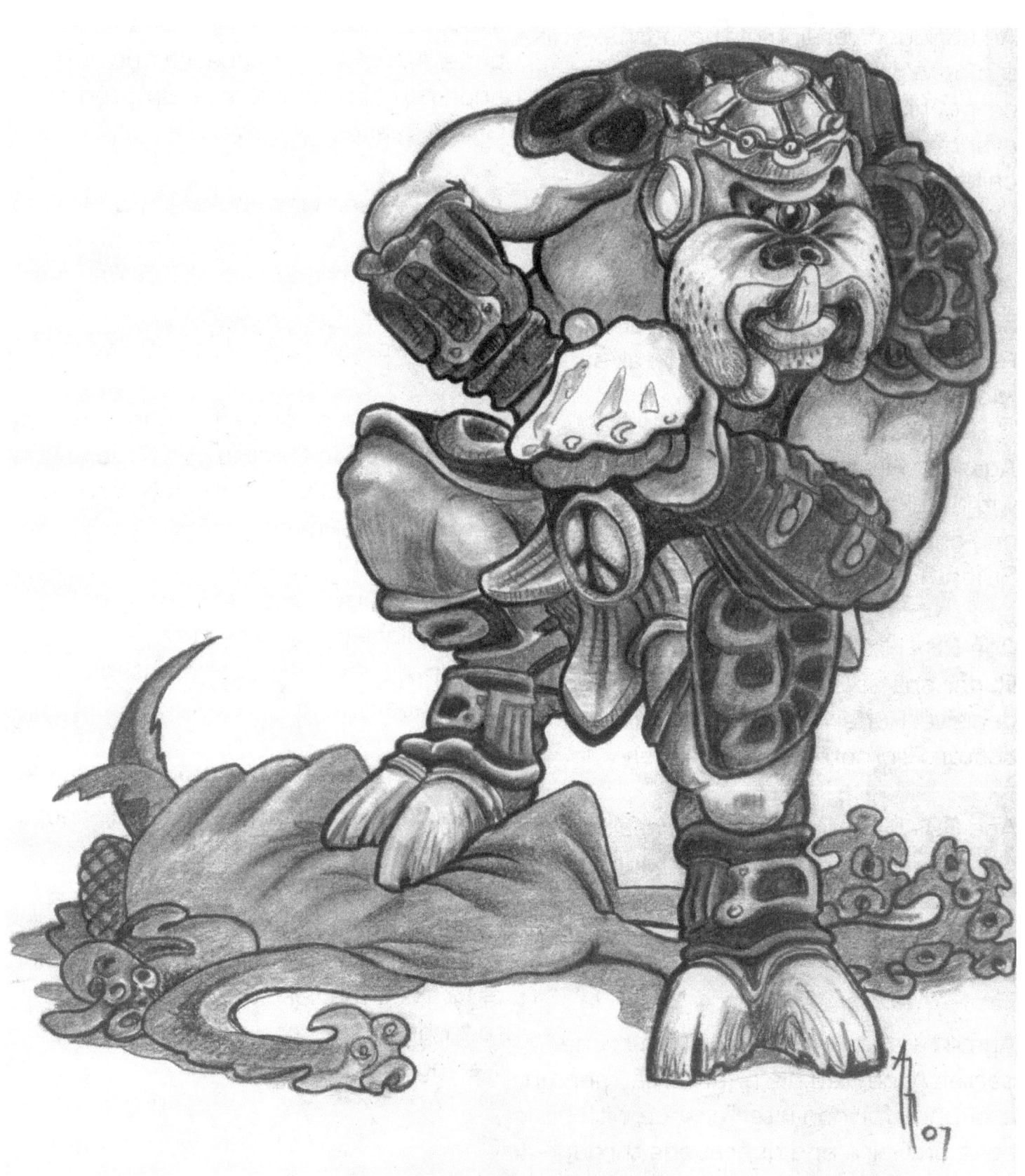

Gelrun Bodyguard

Creator's Commentary on the Gelrun

Every galaxy needs a big dumb brute and the Gelrun definitely fill that role. Sometimes they are fun to play, other times it is fun to easily outwit them since they will likely be used as guards in many sectors of Galaxy Prime. Still, even they can get lucky at times and a few good haymakers can do you in, like the poor pulverized fellow in this artist's rendition. They would appear to be part dog and part bull and their temperment generally matches that assessment as well. They are easily trained but just as easily distracted by shiny or yummy things. And of course their memory is not the greatest. The Drakasians make full use of their limited capabilities, however, and rarely have an issue with it since the Gelrun seem to think that anyone smarter than them is superior to them. It takes a lot to override their commands and training, though, so dont think you can simply convince them to abandon their post and follow your orders instead. The odd thing is that even though they live on a rocky, mountainous planet, they actually make great swimmers. They are not amphibious but with their musculature and stamina they can likely out-paddle any non-aquatic race. They have only reached a Tech level of 2 but not necessarily because of their dim-wittedness. This is mostly because of their brutal dictatorships and their constant clan warfare. They can use weapons and armor but seem to prefer an all-out brawl to settle their differences and to pass the time. Even when they do not fall victim to their own violence, they still have a short lifespan, typically dictated by the length of time it takes that great foretusk of theirs to grow into their eye socket and through their brain. This was a bit of an inside joke between myself and the artist, one which did not reveal itself until the sketch was complete. I have used these guys in several scenarios and they do come off as pretty intimidating. In fact, a Gelrun by the name of Drovell is one of the highest available bounties currently in Galaxy Prime! None of my players or playtesters have had the gumption to try one on as a fully-fledged character. Of course, they are limited in their occupations but why let that stop you? Every game group needs a good tank, right? Honestly, I would like to see someone try to pull off a Gelrun Techie or Xenoscientist, maybe with an awesome mutation, just for fun...

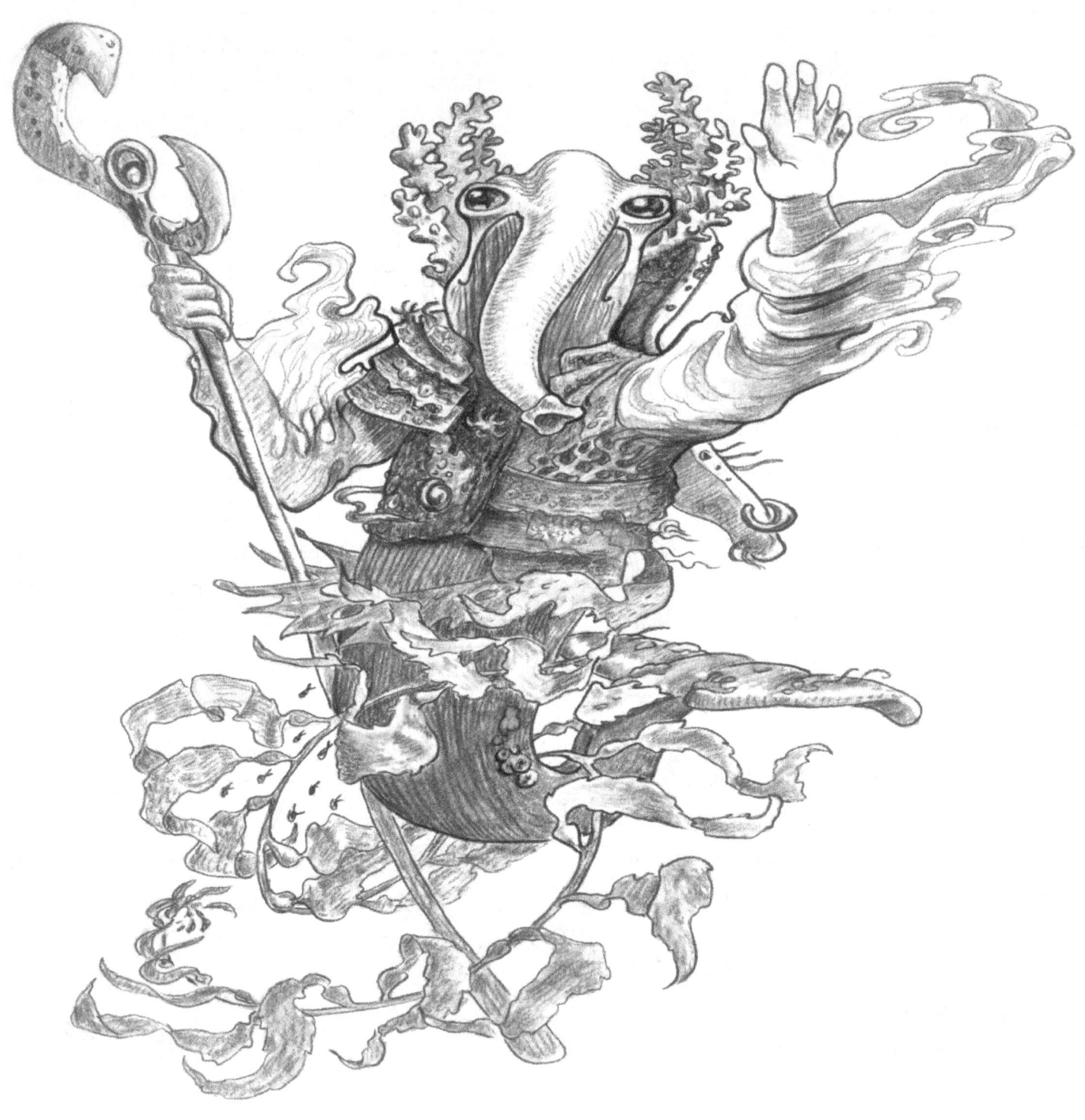

Gilgari Ambassador

Gilgari Poetry

Deep
Deep blue
Deep blue sea
Deep blue sea surrounds
Deep blue sea surrounds me
Deep blue sea surrounds me forever

Beautiful
Beautiful divine
Beautiful divine life
Beautiful divine life thrives
Beautiful divine life thrives gloriously
Beautiful divine life thrives gloriously together

Sacred
Sacred everlasting
Sacred everlasting peace
Sacred everlasting peace soothes
Sacred everlasting peace soothes all
Sacred everlasting peace soothes all minds

Eternal
Eternal pure
Eternal pure love
Eternal pure love protects
Eternal pure love protects sustains
Eternal pure love protects sustains binds

Gluggan Astronomer

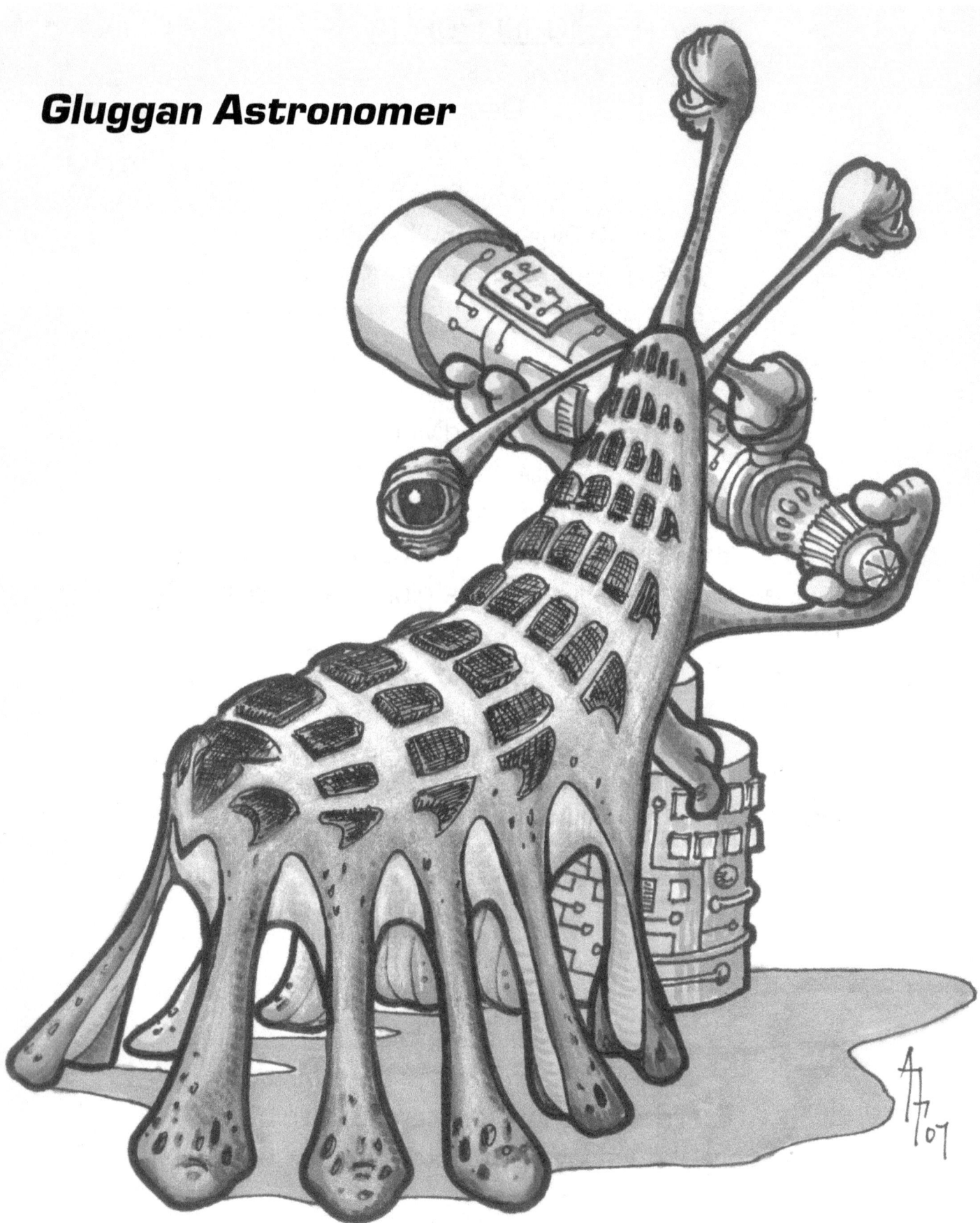

Gluggan Journal

An abridged version of the journal written by G.N.O. activist Oobul with excerpts highlighting some of her achievements in her crusade to protect and preserve the natural resources and endangered lifeforms of Galaxy Prime.

Age 1 - Accidently discovered an underground cavern teeming with flora and fauna. Helped to divert water from a small lake found there into arid regions which subsequently became lush!

Age 2 - Gathered a large cluster of zib worms and distributed them to barren areas in order to revitalize the soil and plant life there.

Age 3 - My hydroponic garden is the most beautiful and successful on all of Gulga! Many awards won and accolades received.

Age 4 - Traveled to Suulva to study new scientific methods of environmental conservation.

Age 5 - Created offspring!

Age 6 - Witnessed a Kunlaati attack. They were angry that we had naught but plants and animals in our cargo hold.

Age 7 - Visited the enormous planet of Den-sar. Such a cornucopia of plant and animal life here!

Age 8 - Helped form the Guardians of Natural Order. Now our knowledge and methodologies can be focused and spread throughout Galaxy Prime. We can help so many worlds avoid starvation, deforestation and extinction!

Age 9 - G.N.O headquarters set up on newly discovered world of Plavia in the largely unexplored Frontier Sector.

Age 10 - Made contact with sentient plant life on Plavia!

Age 11 - Lost an eye in a wind storm. Ouch!

Age 12 - Found allies in the Lycanthians, an animalistic shapeshifting race native to the Frontier.

Age 13 - Helped to rescue several Snoggan refugees who had no home after their sun exploded. Poor people!

Age 14 - Very ill. Must have absorbed some nasty pollen...

(Oobul died of this sickness, aged 14.)

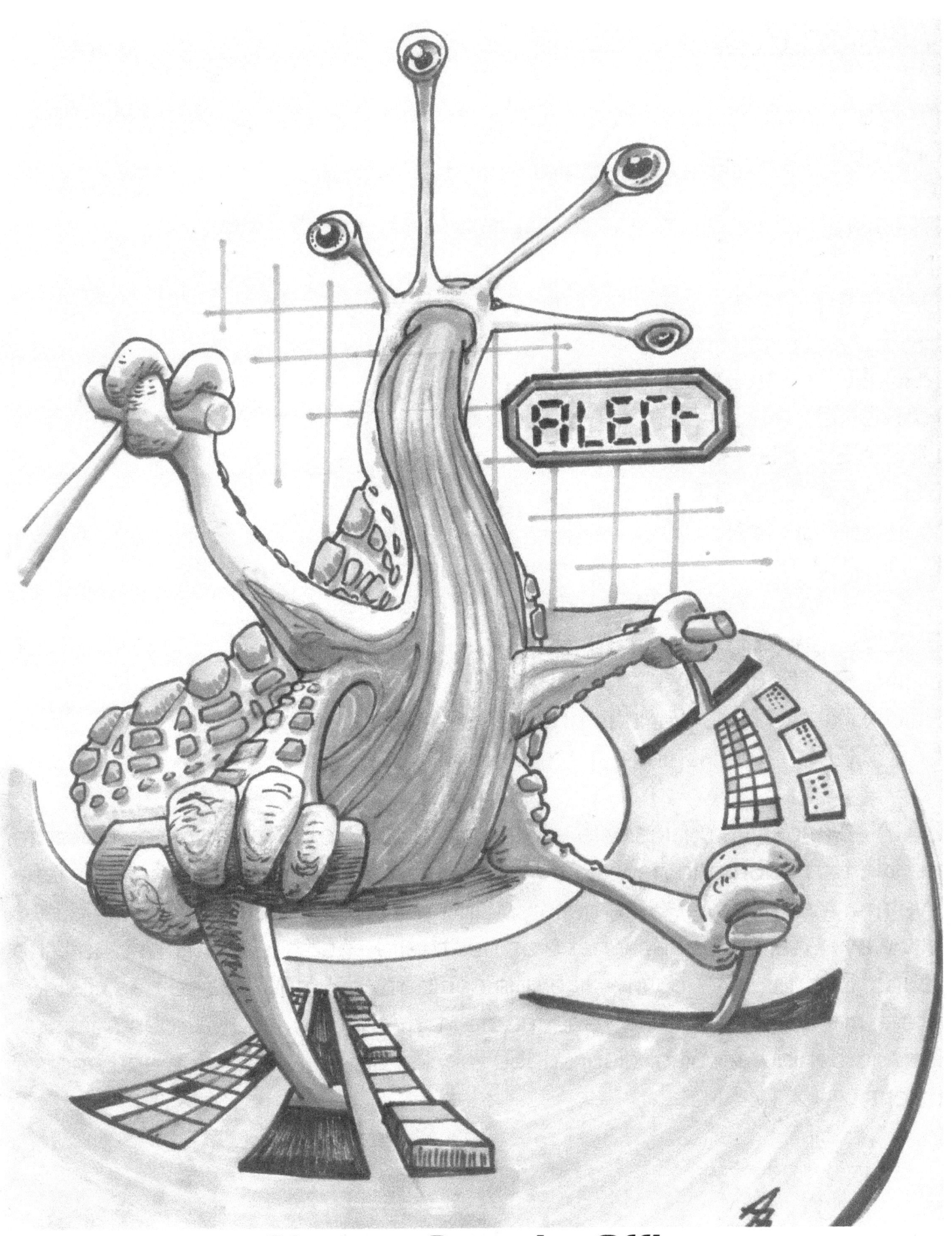

Gluggan Security Officer

Wanted Poster

NAME - Oravia
SPECIES - Grenyan

STRENGTH - 14
INTELLIGENCE - 18
DEXTERITY - 22
SPEED - 66
PROJECTILE WEAPONS - 70
HAND TO HAND - 66
DEFENSE - 62
OBSERVATION - 64
WILLFORCE - 52
LUCK - 54

SKILLS - Stealth, Market, Social
CRIMES - Theft, Fraud
BOUNTY - 50,000 (various private citizens); Alive
LAST SEEN - Kor Regime

DATA - Obsessive curiosity is a killer, especially for Oravia. In her quest for new information and new experiences she has lost her tail, lost her left eye and lost her way. She merely wanted to explore Galaxy Prime in every way possible, to see what was out there and to learn from what she found. Of course, a journey like this costs money and so she had to lie, steal, cheat, grift, con and seduce her way through the various sectors, leaving behind a trail of disgruntled marks, bankrupted saps and angry lovers.

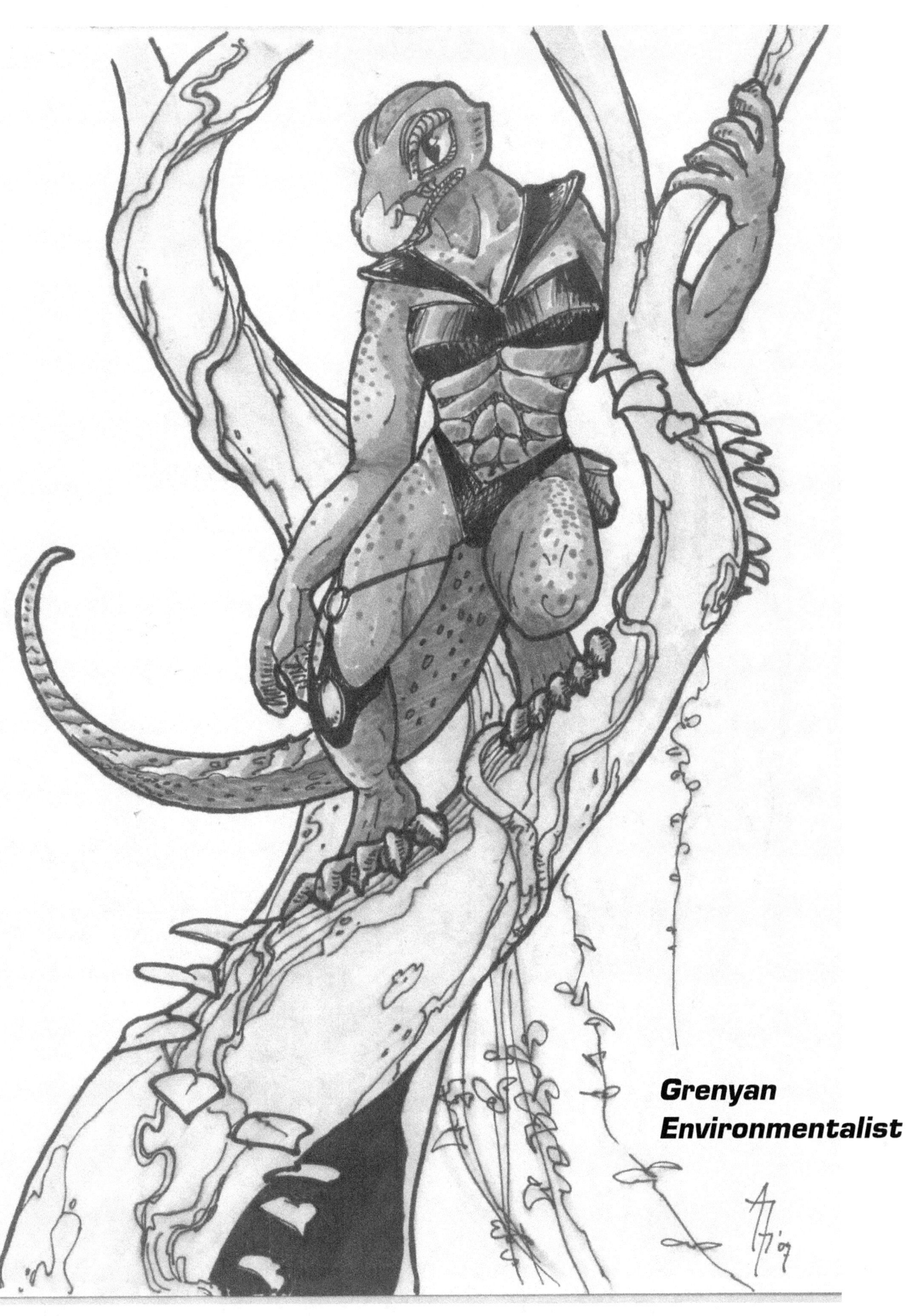

Grenyan
Environmentalist

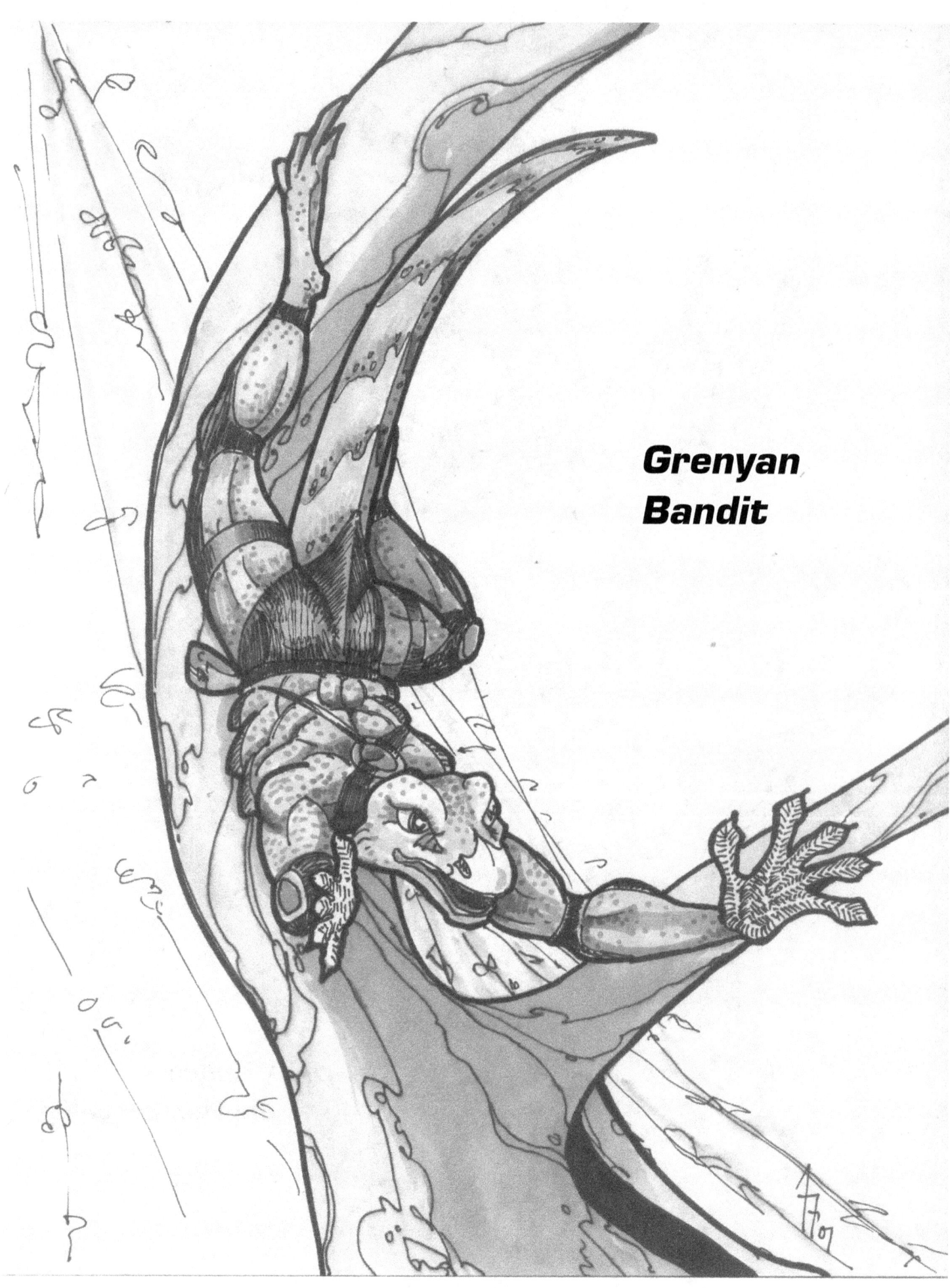

Grenyan
Bandit

Izars Mercenaries

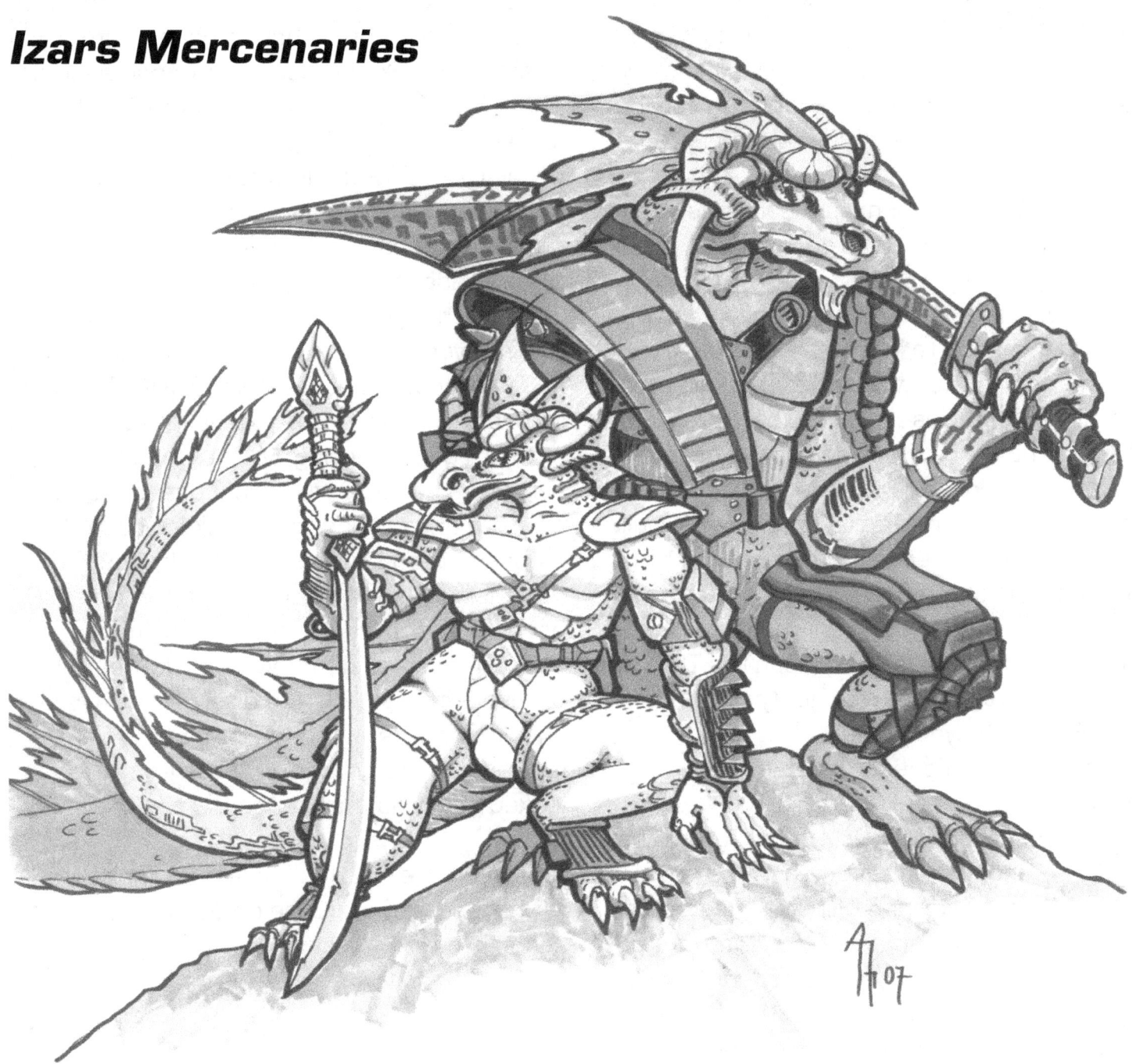

"I dont see what the big deal is," said my sub-draconix. "These Orgars die just like anything else!"

He finished emptying the clip of his pulse rifle into the corpse of the massive orgar, though the thing was already dead.

"Conserve your ammo, fool," I reprimanded my sub-draconix. "We still have many more yet to deal with!"

The tail and tongue of my sub-draconix flicked not so much in frustration at my comment as in anticipation of the work ahead. He was hotheaded and rash but always got the job done. And this job was just like a hundred others before it. Apparently, some Exomech vessel had crash landed on the Orgar world and we were hired by our Thasian "masters" to go retrieve the remains. Not of the people, mind you, but the cyberware and other technology that was so superfluously integrated into their pathetic little bodies. Why the Exomech were hanging around this primitive world was anybody's guess but it really didn't matter. My job –the job I was well paid to do– was simply to get in, destroy any resistance and get out with the cargo. A simple matter overall, but obviously too difficult for a Thasian.

As Chief Draconix of my platoon I had eagerly taken the job, anxious to see some action and needing to keep my soldiers in a high state of readiness at all times. I had been hoping to get a chance to kill some Runarians or some Kor, as that would present a greater challenge but these dull neanderthals would have to do for now. I could see why lesser species would fear the Orgars; they were easily over 6.5 meters tall and had the bulk to match. However, lacking technology and the intelligence to use it made them little more than big, fat targets. Come to think of it, perhaps that was the reason the Thasians didn't want the Orgars to get their hands on the Exomech cyberware...

"Main vessel up ahead!" cried my sub-draconix.

As we marched forward, I could see the bulk of the mangled starship...and it was crawling with Orgars! They had turned the corvette-class vehicle into some sort of living complex and the area was strewn with debris and garbage, partly from the crash and partly from the Orgar inspection of the site. I began to see them playing with drones, bots and bits of cyberware and they obviously had no concept of what to do with it. The zone was overrun with these giant meatheads, some inside the ship, making a direct assault impossible, at least if we wanted to recover the tech in working order.

"Form up, you wyrm-tongued wonders!" I ordered and my platoon fell rapidly into place. "Unfortunately, we cant just bomb the sods with explosives," I explained and there was a collective sigh of disappointment. "But we can gas the place until every single one of them drops dead!" That brought a cheer from my loyal troops. "So don your masks and encircle the site. On my mark we pump 'em full of fumes!"

My platoon moved out expertly, forming a nice, tight cordon around the ship. Once their fume masks were in place, I raised my grenade launcher for all to see. The Orgars either hadn't noticed us yet or were too involved to care. I pulled the trigger and my weapon made a satisfying THUMP as it lobbed the poisonous explosive into the midst of the Orgar gathering. My platoon followed suit and a double-dozen grenades found their way into and around the wrecked vessel. Clouds of red fumes began to billow out of the enclosure and howls of surprise and fury emanated from the center of the chaos. We waited several moments and when the crimson smoke began to dissipate we were shocked at what we saw: not a single Orgar lay dead on the ground. In fact they merely looked angry as they began to stalk towards us.

"Looks like we get to charge our employers for a little bit of overtime on this one," I remarked with a wicked grin.

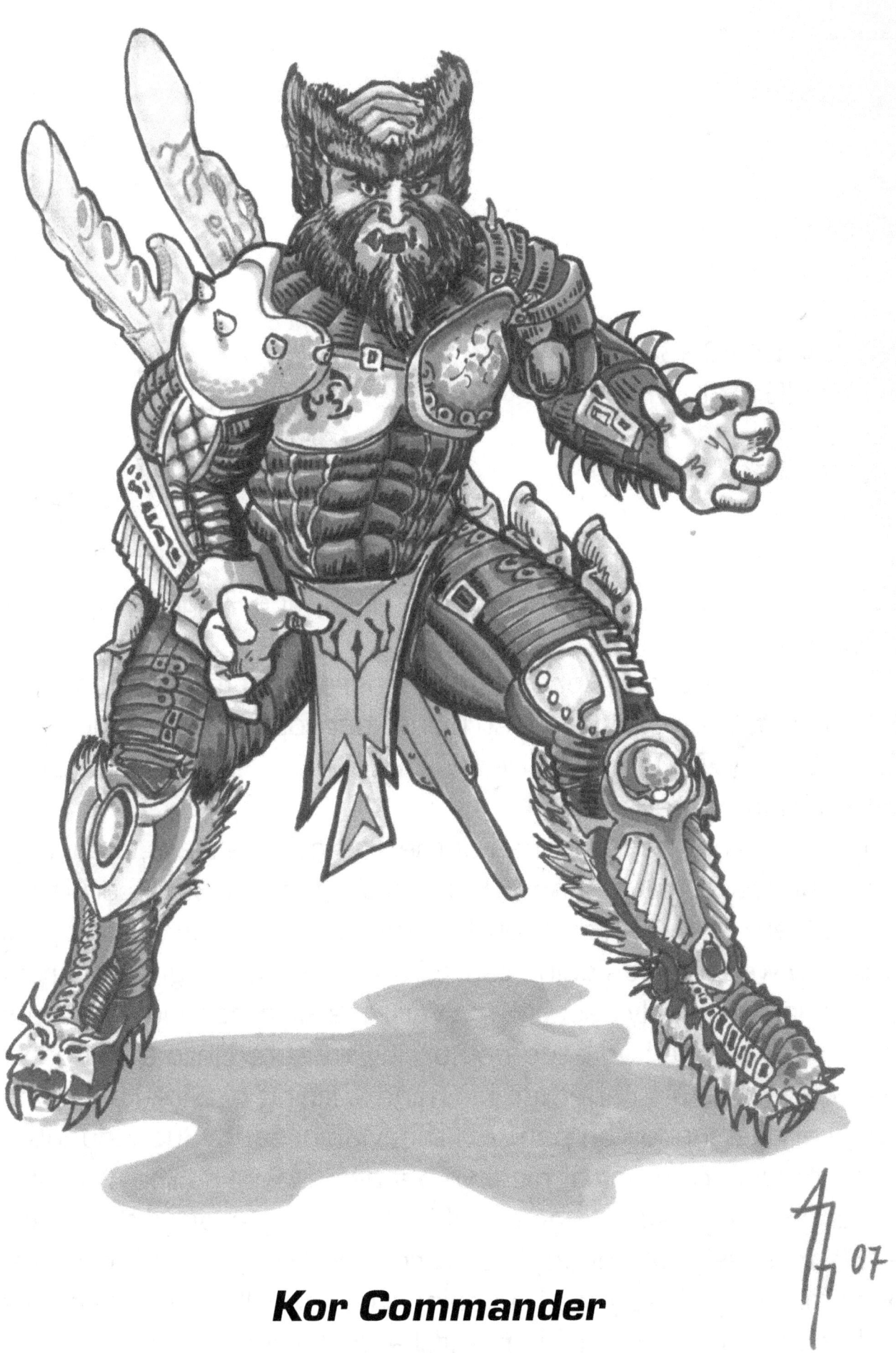

Kor Commander

Wanted Poster

NAME - Kodrot
SPECIES - Kor
STRENGTH - 28
INTELLIGENCE - 17
DEXTERITY - 16
SPEED - 48
PROJECTILE WEAPONS - 73
HAND TO HAND - 84
DEFENSE - 55
OBSERVATION - 51
WILLFORCE - 95
LUCK - 61
MUTATIONS - Adaptation, Body Weaponry, Carapace, Regeneration, Superior Strength
DEFECTS - Stench, Vestigial Appendage, Vulnerability (Tox-weapons)
CRIMES - Murder, War Crimes, Destruction of property, Desertion
BOUNTY - 1,000,000; Dead or Alive; KOR REGIME, TRIUMVIRATE SPACE
LAST SEEN - Triumvirate Space
DATA - Kodrot was on the front lines of the Triumvirate wars, a shining example of Kor bravery and honor. Then, battle damage to his cruiser resulted in a freak explosion that left him changed forever. Some speculate that a new weapon was being tested and that he caught the brunt of its discharge. The highly decorated War-master emerged alive from the conflagration but he had become horribly mutated into a being of raw power. Sadly, this also affected his mind, turning him into a psychopathic force of destruction on par with the Malboreans. Subsequently he began to massacre many of his own people, as well as the Sovaari, Zhani, Gilgari and any one else he could find roaming around that sector of space. He was last seen heading towards the Mordas, with rumors of his motives following closely; was he going there to kill the dark entity, to kill himself or to find a cure for his mental and physical state?

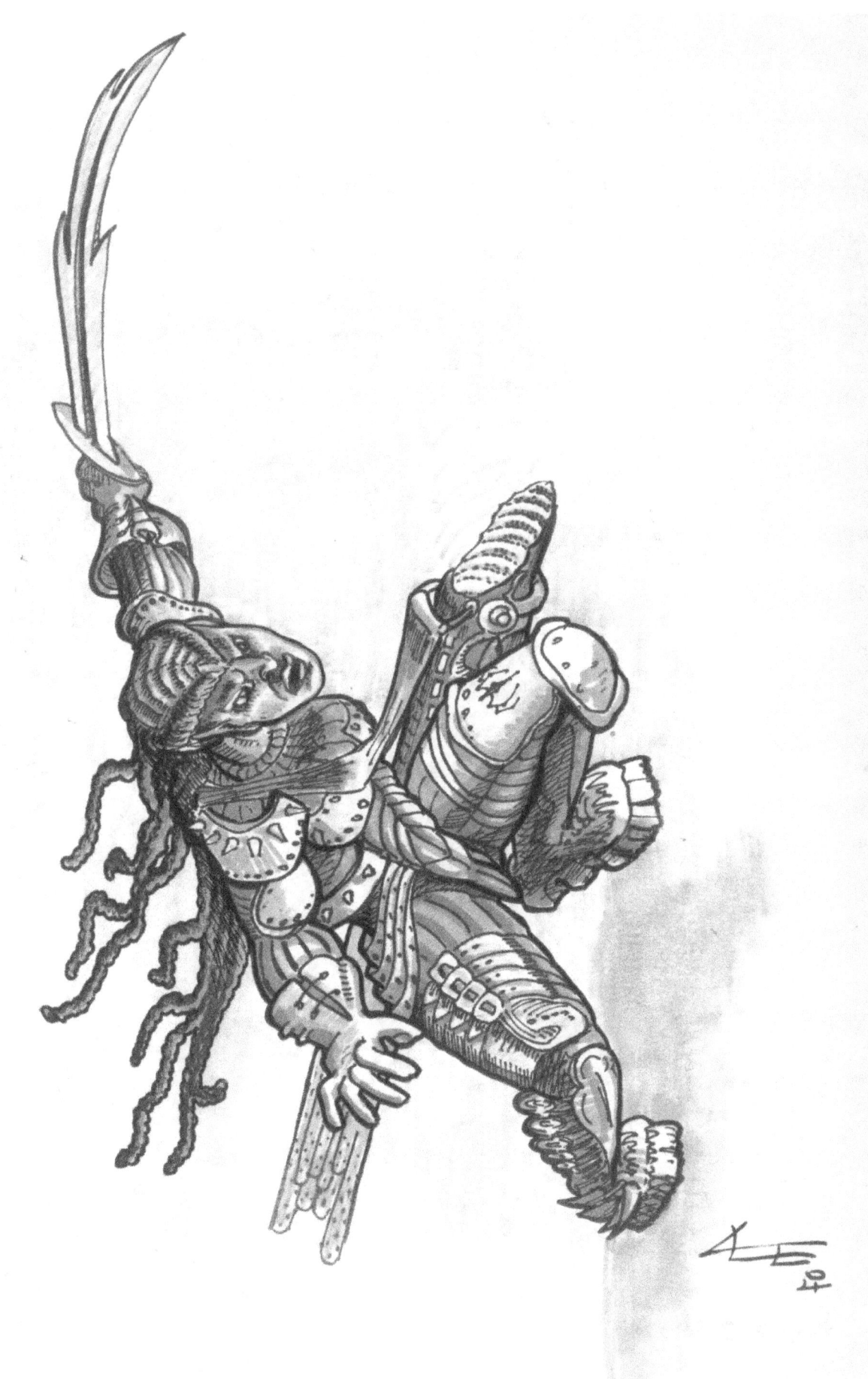

Kor Warrior

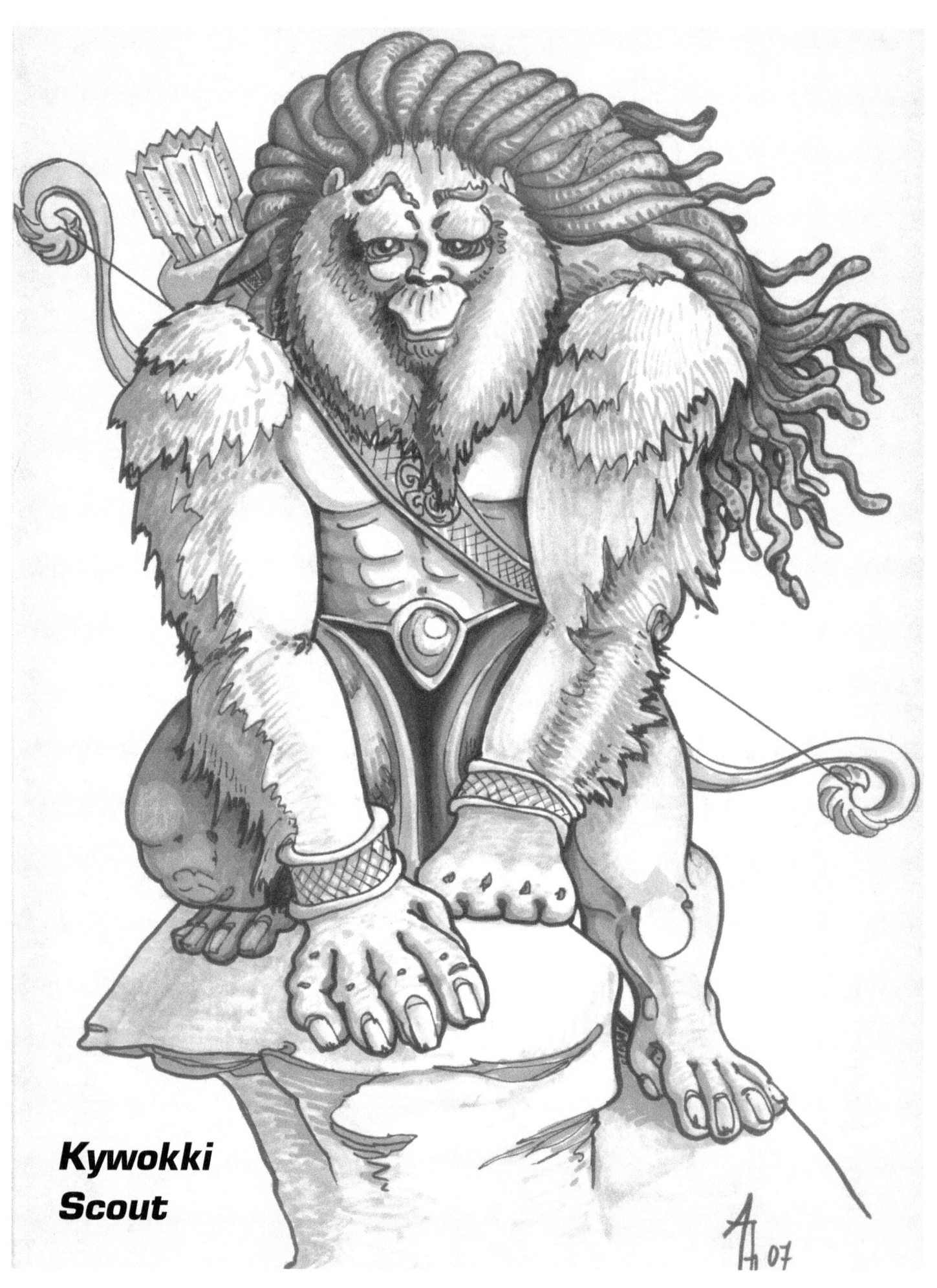

Kywokki
Scout

Kywokki Poem

Up and down
Up and down
Tree to tree
Tree to tree
Green and brown
Green and brown
Must be free
Must be free
Hunter's role
Hunter's role
Seek them out
Seek them out
Reach the goal
Reach the goal
Triumphant shout
Triumphant shout
Family life
Family life
Protect the home
Protect the home
End the strife
End the strife
Free to roam
Free to roam
Sun to rise
Sun to rise
Sun to set
Sun to set
Freedom's prize
Freedom's prize
Honor met
Honor met

L'kri Diplomats

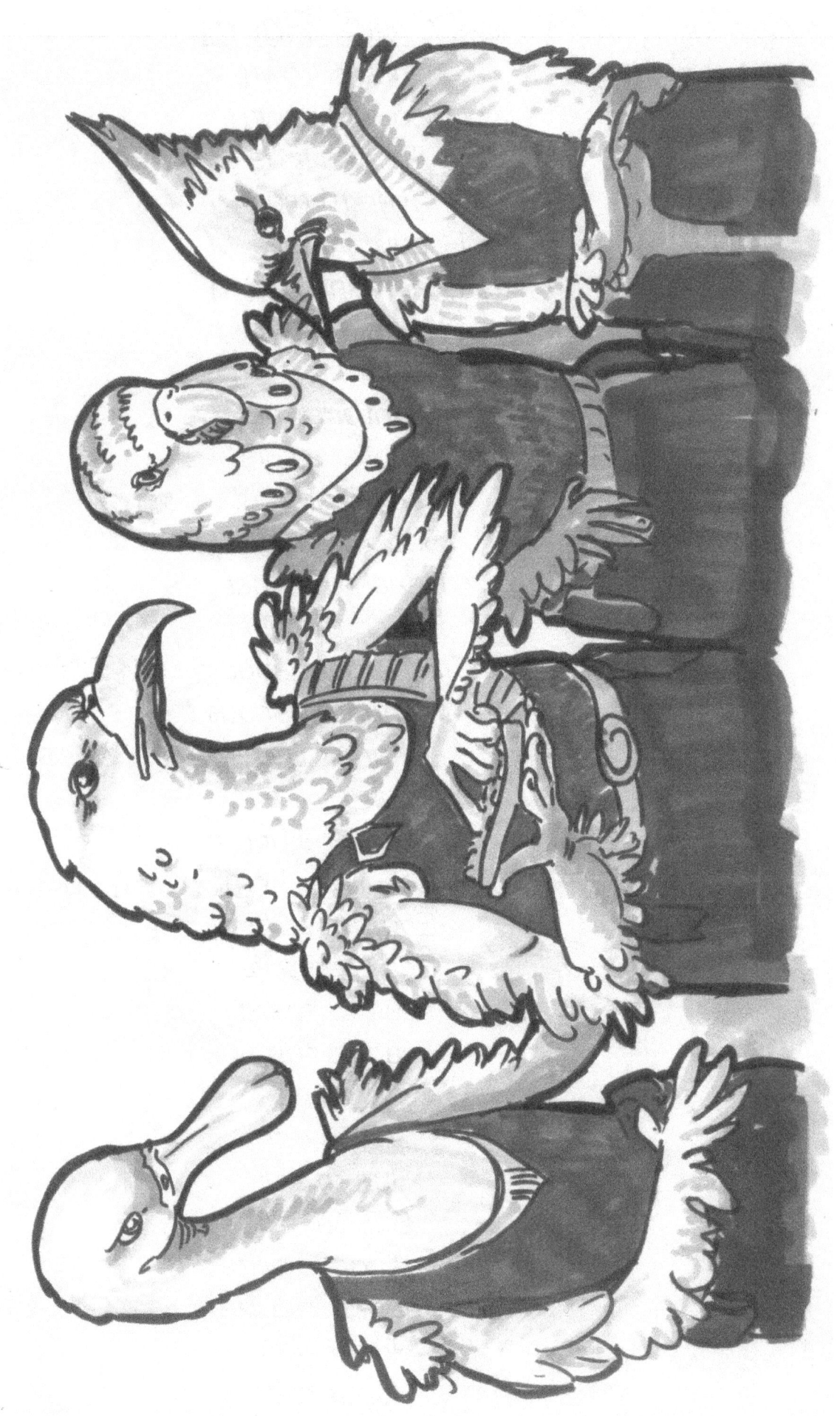

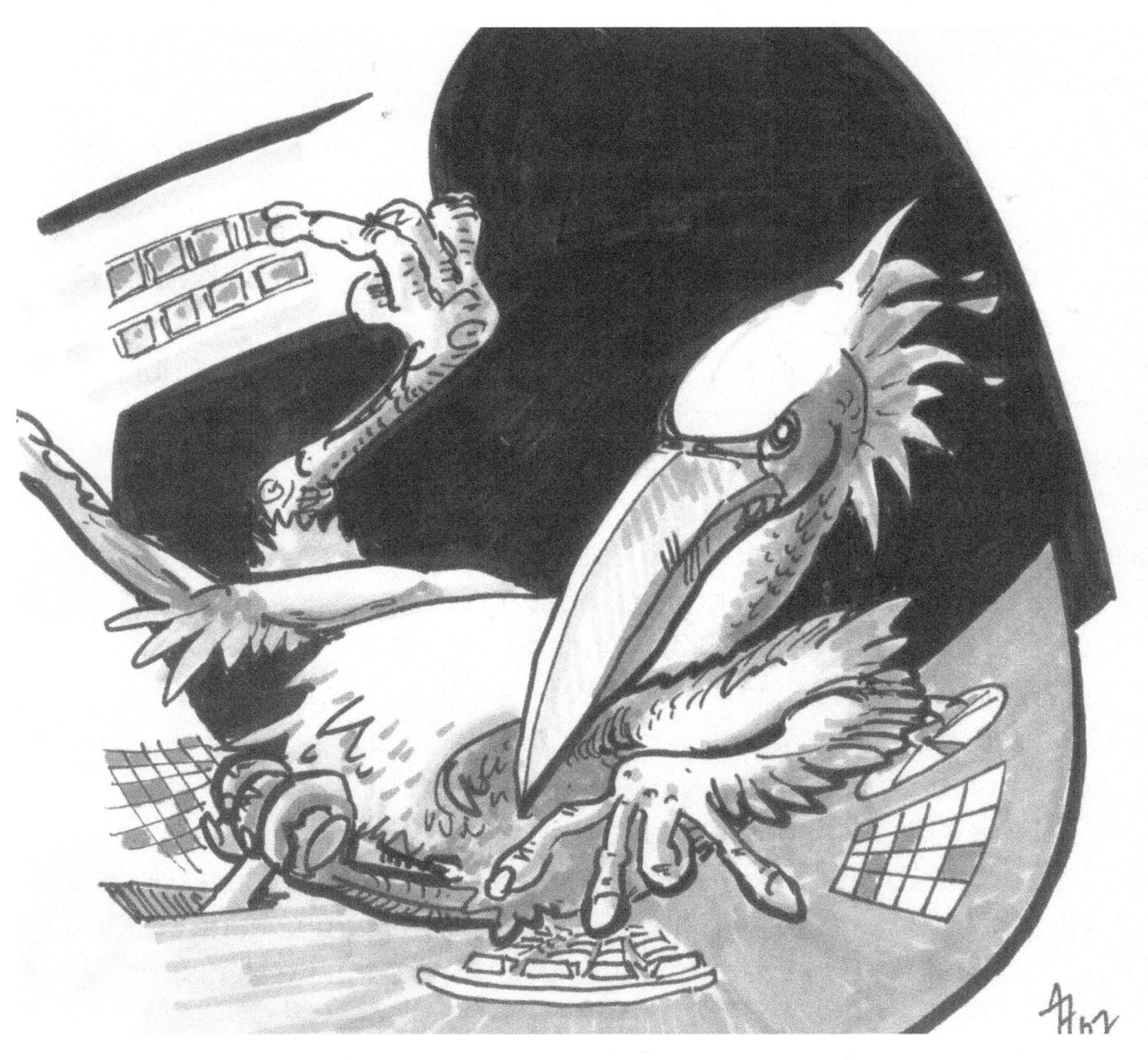

L'kri Pilot

Expanded L'kri Timeline

1M6C - Lkrian flocks begin to consolidate and build sky cities

2M4C - Work begins on mechanical flying apparatus for flightless Lkri

2M8C - First contact with Arn

3M - Religion banned planetwide

3M3C - Grengi shuttle Lkri to second planet in system and assist their colonization efforts...for a price

3M7C - Sulven help Lkri with technology; society advances quickly

4M2C - Waves of Kraa hunters invade Lkrian worlds; fierce battles and many casualties on both sides

4M5C - A whole generation of sterile eggs; massive drop in population

4M9C - Kunlaati prey on secondary Lkrian world; instant enmity formed

5M3C - Hypergates brought to homeworld

5M6C - Internal crime rates drop to almost nil

5M8C - Limij infestation causes massive droughts

6M2C - First contact with Nomme; treaties achieved

6M5C - Lkri exchange Grengi for Molgans as primary trade partners

6M7C - Sulven League formed with Lkri as charter members

7M - Democratic government replaced by autocrat

7M4C - Avian flu takes toll on both Lkrian worlds

7M9C - First Kinet among populace

8M3C - Threats by Tuth crimelords repulsed; entire Tuth clan wiped out

8M6C - Lkri begin purchasing fleets of starships from around the galaxy

9M2C - Lkrian Law Syndicate formed; Lkri take to space to dispense justice

9M7C - Lkri aid Drakasians and Buthari in their bid for freedom from the Runarian yoke

10M1C - Rogue asteroids from Thuun Belt on a collision course for the homeworld are destroyed; Runarian/Tuth involvement suspected

10M5C - Lkri decline membership in galactic council

11M - Lkrian fleet dispatched to fight Mordas is never heard from again

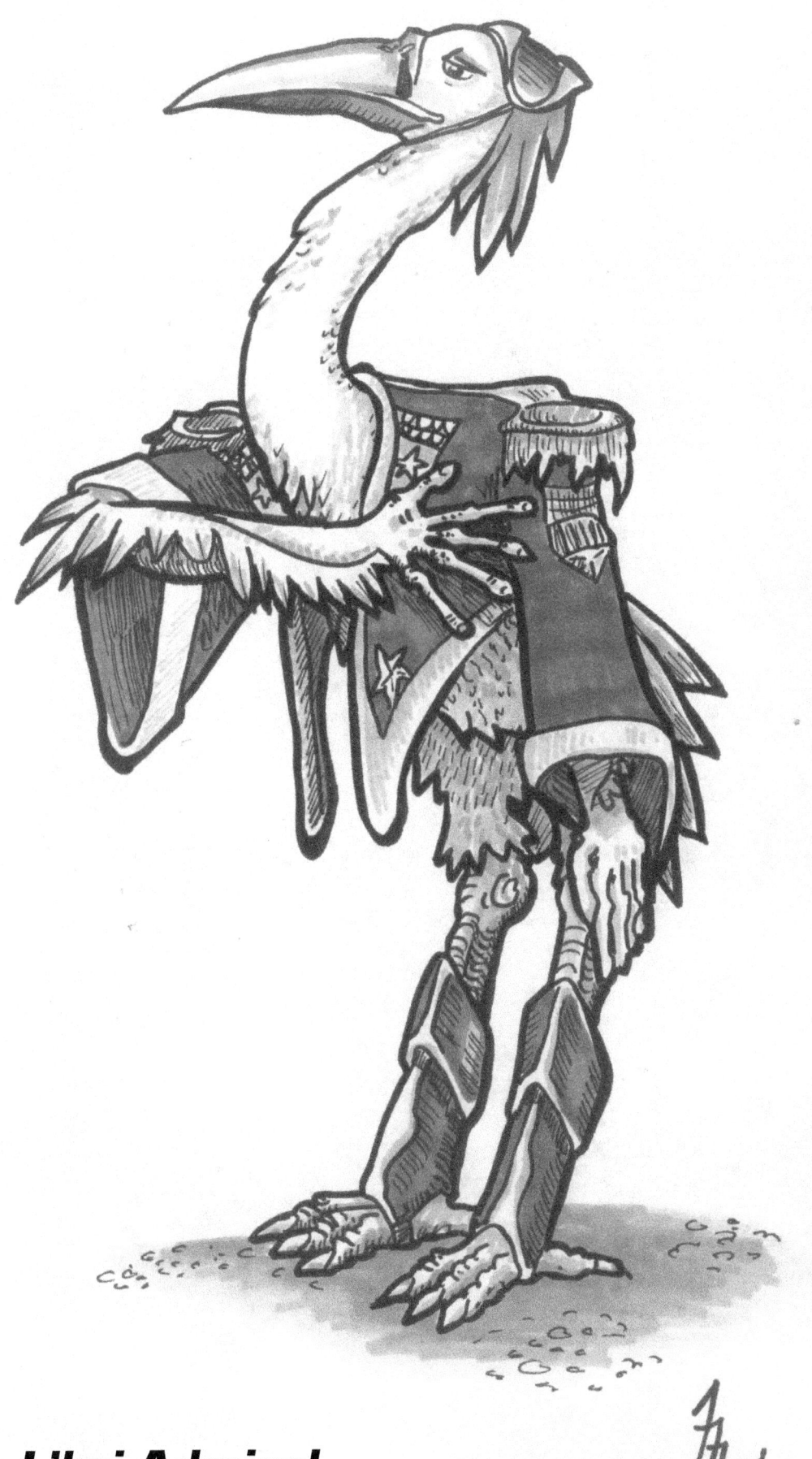

L'kri Admiral

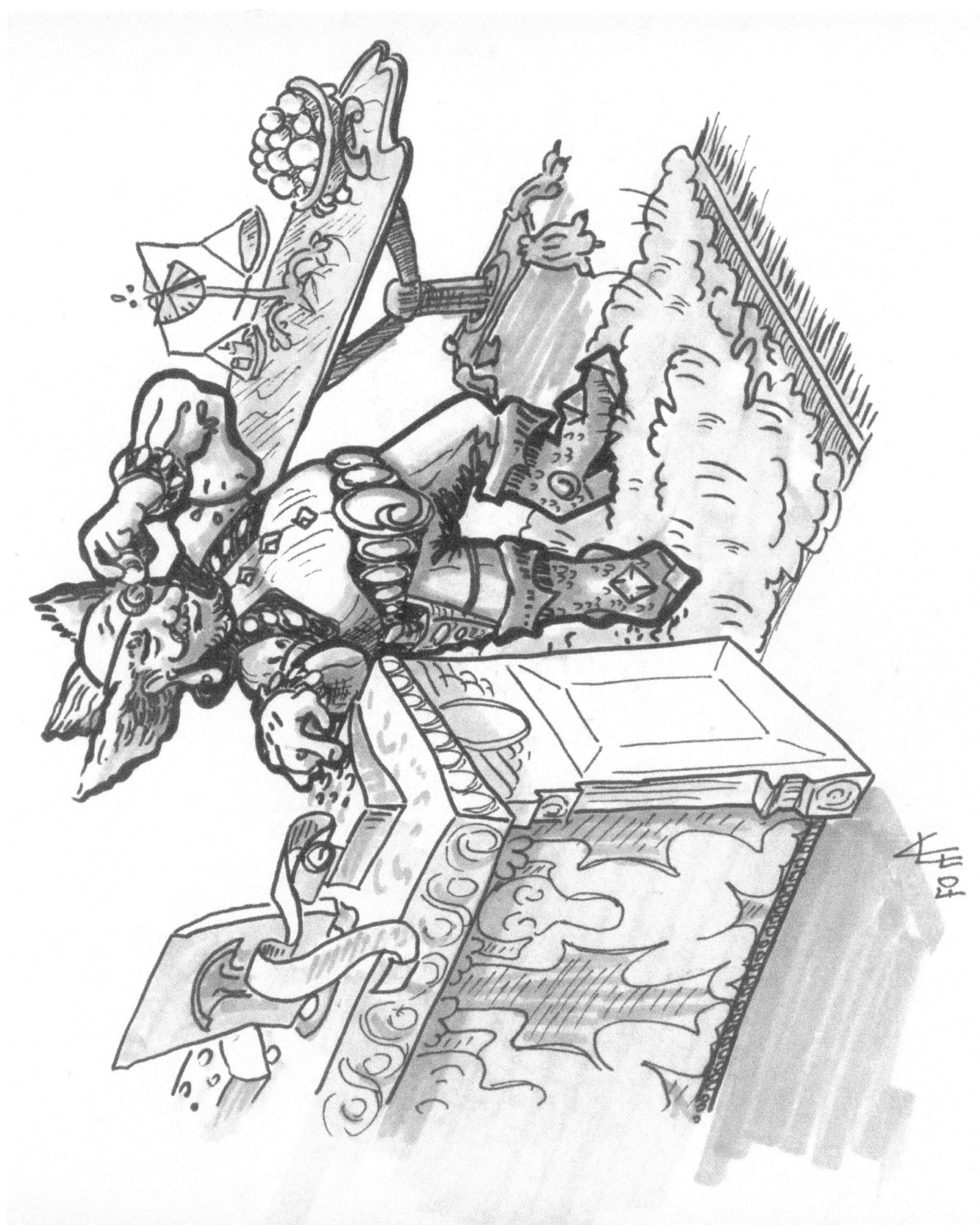

Molgan Trader

Quoth the Molgan

Dead or alive, in stasis or in chains, you're coming with me!

Two days ago I saw a cruiser that could haul that barquadontus. If you want to get out of here you talk to me.

I will not drink beer. Beer is the mindkiller.

Just remember: no matter what wormhole you go through, there you are.

It will be a dangerous place, but it will also be our last, best hope to defeat the Mordas.

If it oozes we can kill it.

It cant rain all the time...unless you're on Den-sar.

Listen up you primitive Detheks! This is my tox-gun!

Anything that moves is a Gelrun. Anything that stands still is a well-trained Gelrun!

Fighting against the Kor is indeed a strange game. The only winning move is not to play.

We're gonna need a bigger gunboat...

I love it when my clan comes together!

I'm two days from retirement and I'm getting too old for this ship!

By Graeton's gauntlet, by the moons of Molgada, I shall avenge thee!

Two in the cargo hold, ready to go. We be fast and they be slow!

They may take our wives but they can never take our credsticks!

Release the Gexran!

What is best in life? To crush your enemies, to see them driven before you and to hear the sound of their Q*drives exploding!

Norgh Lawmen

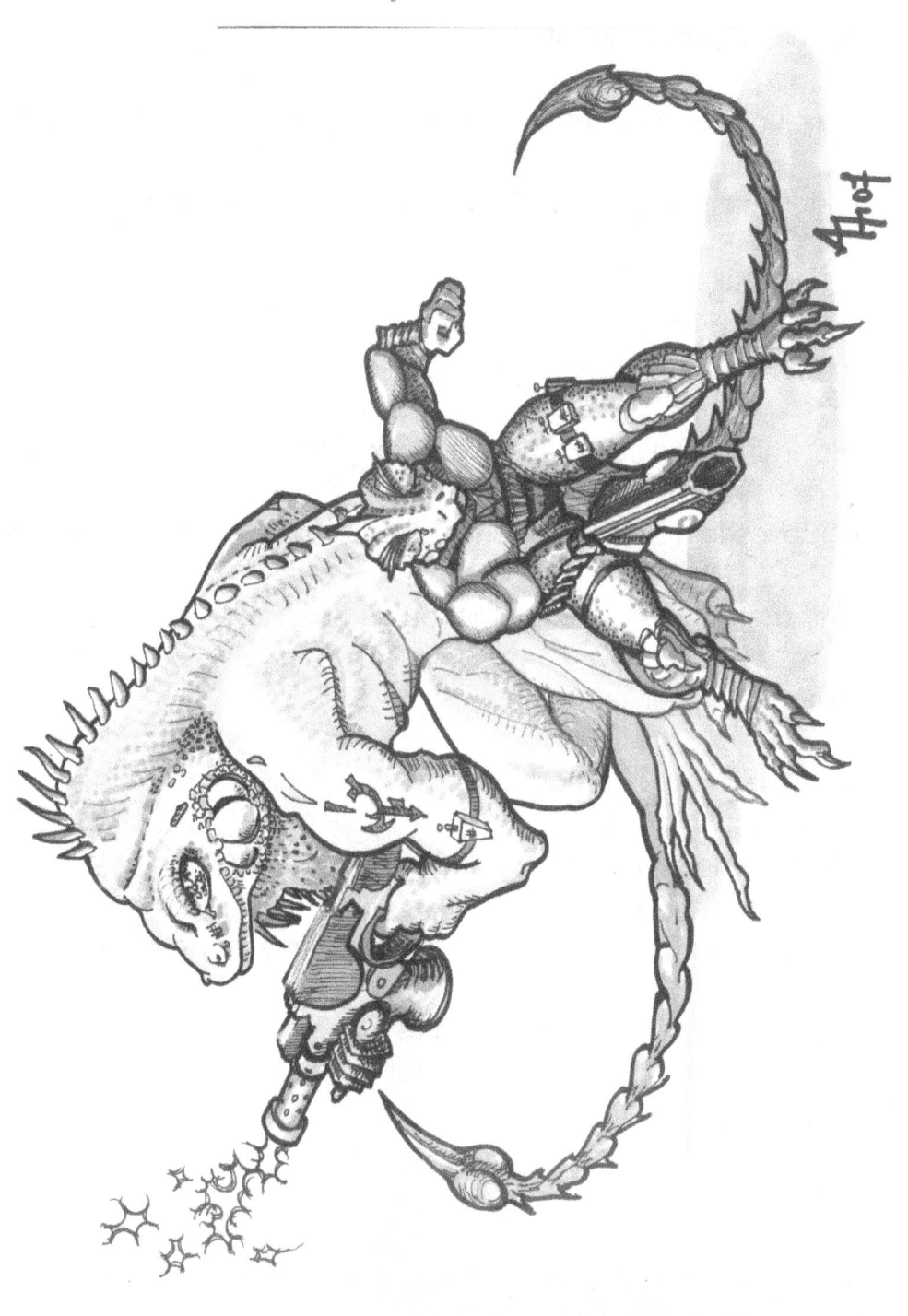

Tale of the Norgh

"Drung build this. Drung fix that. Just because Drung is a techie doesn't mean he doesn't have other things to do!"

Drung's mate looked at Drung. Drung was upset. Drung was more upset than the time the Thasians came and repossessed his sand sled. What was wrong with Drung? Was it Drung's job? Was it Drung's offspring? Was it Drung's tummy again? It couldn't be Drung's mate. Drung's mate did everything Drung's mate was supposed to do, sometimes over and over. No, something else was bothering Drung and Drung's mate was determined to find out what it was.

"What is bothering Drung?" asked Drung's mate.

"If Drung's mate doesn't know," Drung replied, "then Drung isn't going to tell Drung's mate!"

Drung's mate was shocked. Drung has never spoken to Drung's mate this way before.

"Should Drung's mate leave Drung alone?" asked Drung's mate.

Drung didn't answer. Drung was not being helpful.

"Perhaps Drung should go away for a while," offered Drung's mate.

Drung left.

Well, that was easy, thought Drung's mate.

Drung walked for hours. Drung knew where he wanted to go. Drung finally arrived at the tallest dune on all of Norgh. Drung climbed that dune and sat on a flat rock, curling up and absorbing its warmth and the heat of the setting suns. Drung looked around. Drung saw no one. Drung liked this place. It was Drung's favorite. Drung could get away from it all here. Drung needed to be away from it all right now. Drung had a problem. Drung took off his work vest, filled with tools. Drung had been using them to build and fix Q*drives for the last 7 years but Drung was not well paid for his work. Drung did dangerous work, being exposed to quantum radiation on a daily basis. Drung should be paid better for his efforts. Drung set down his vest and reached for his back. Drung could feel the vestigial appendages protruding there. Drung held his breath and strained. Drung could feel them move slightly, unfolding just enough to be recognizable as small wings. Norgh weren't supposed to have wings! Drung didn't like them. Drung thought they were ugly. Drung knew that they would never be big enough to carry his bulky form through the sky. Drung knew that the radiation has caused this. Drung wanted to get rid of them before someone saw them. Drung grabbed his plasma torch from his vest. Drung ignited it and aimed it at his left wing.

"Parent, don't!"

Drung whirled at the cry. Drung saw Drung's offspring.

"What is Drung's offspring doing here?" he asked. "Drung did not see Drung's offspring following him."

"Drung's offspring followed parent," said Drung's offspring. "Drung's offspring was worried about parent."

"But how did Drung's offspring get here without Drung noticing?"

"Drung's offspring has a secret too," replied Drung's offspring.

Drung watched as his offspring suddenly changed colors to match the surrounding sand, becoming nearly invisible. Drung was shocked.

"Drung's offspring likes parent's wings," said the younger Norgh. "Will parent keep them?"

Drung thought for a moment. "Drung will keep them," Drung said at length. "And Drung and his offspring will keep their secrets together."

Drung's offspring changed back to his normal greenish hue and embraced his parent.

And Drung was happy.

Reeyarian Musician

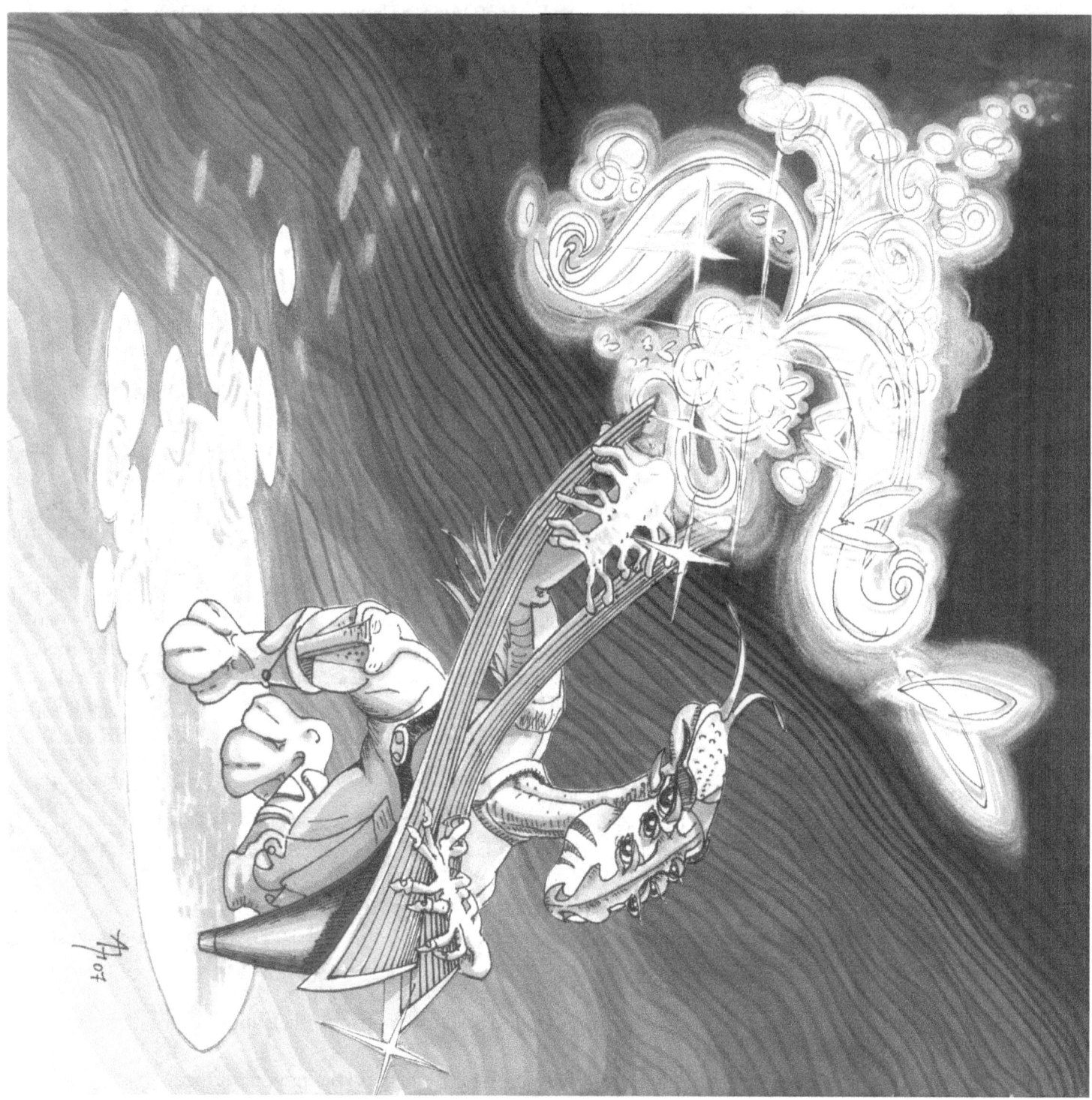

Lyrics of the Reeyar

With strings and lights
I make my way
I cross the stars
To make my pay

With throngs of fans
And hanger's-on
I ply my trade
And sing my song

To every stage
And bar unknown
Cantina's strange
And D.M. zone

Females flock
They push and shove
Just one chance
To get my love

I write the words
I play the tunes
On lively planets
On barren moons

Hop the freighter
Wormhole flight
Rock all day
Party all night

Hear the music
See the show
Cant stay long
It's time to go

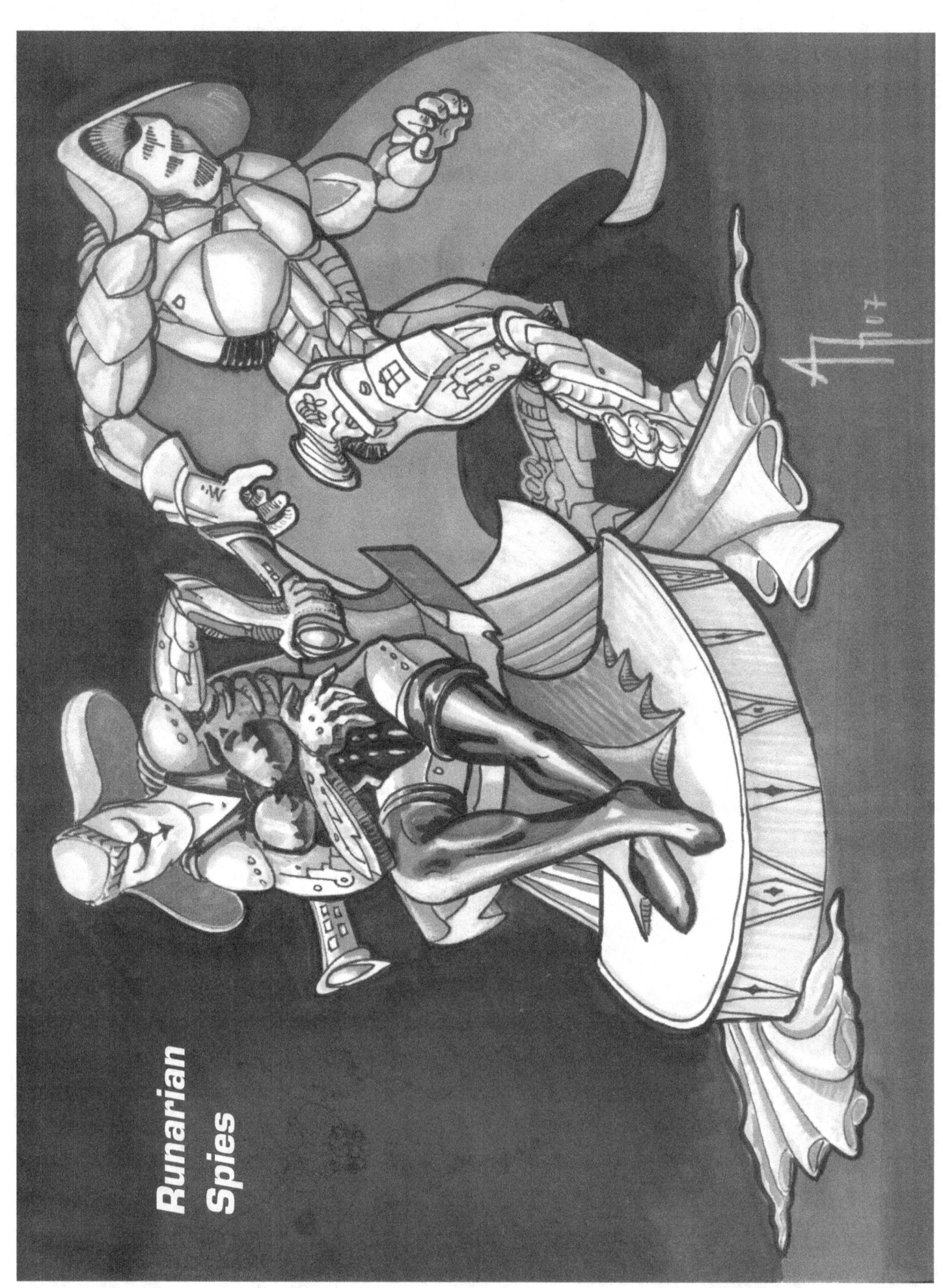

Runarian
Spies

Analysis of recent Runarian activity presented to the Galactic Council as compiled by the Triumvirate Security Service

Illegal blockade of Buthari homeworld continues but shows signs of weakening due to efforts of the Buthari resistance, the TSS and other independent elements. Runarian ~~vessels~~ remain at the cutting edge of technology due to advanced research techniques and acts of theft/espionage committed against other technological species, such as the ~~Exomech~~, the Nomme, the ~~Salven~~, the ~~Thasians~~ and the ~~Iron~~. All weapons, armor, equipment, drones, bots and cyberware also rated at the highest levels of efficacy. Tactics are constantly evolving and changing though the overall strategy remains constant, that of domination of individual worlds then entire sectors. Use of ~~hypergates~~ and ~~wormholes~~, even uncharted and unstable ones, is a frequent occurence. This practice is key to many of their missions and often leads to a higher success rate, based on speed of travel and the element of surprise. Recommend higher security at all such locales. Infiltration into the highest levels of government is probable on the following worlds: Crux, Klaat, Dlabba, Muot, Riin, Shingrah, Dioba, ~~Kur~~, ~~Nomme~~, Tauris, ~~Saalva~~. Experimentation with creating ~~mutants~~ and/or ~~Kinet~~ amongst the populace continues with varying degrees of success. Frequently, this is without the knowledge or permission of the subject. Runarian agents avoid discovery at all costs and when discovered the use of force is even eschewed in favor of escape. However, when combat is unavoidable, the use of lethal force becomes unrestrained. The capture and subsequent interrogation of Runarian agents remains difficult due to the multiple redundant ~~suicide~~ devices built into their gear and outfits. Masks remain immovable as it destroys their face and any hope of individual recognition. One xenomorph, the ~~Dioban Antiron~~, appears to have a severe psychological effect upon all Runarians, though the cause is as yet undetermined. Observation of Runarians in proximity to this entity has uncovered an all-consuming, irrational fear of the life form and Runarians will lose all decorum in the face of its presence.

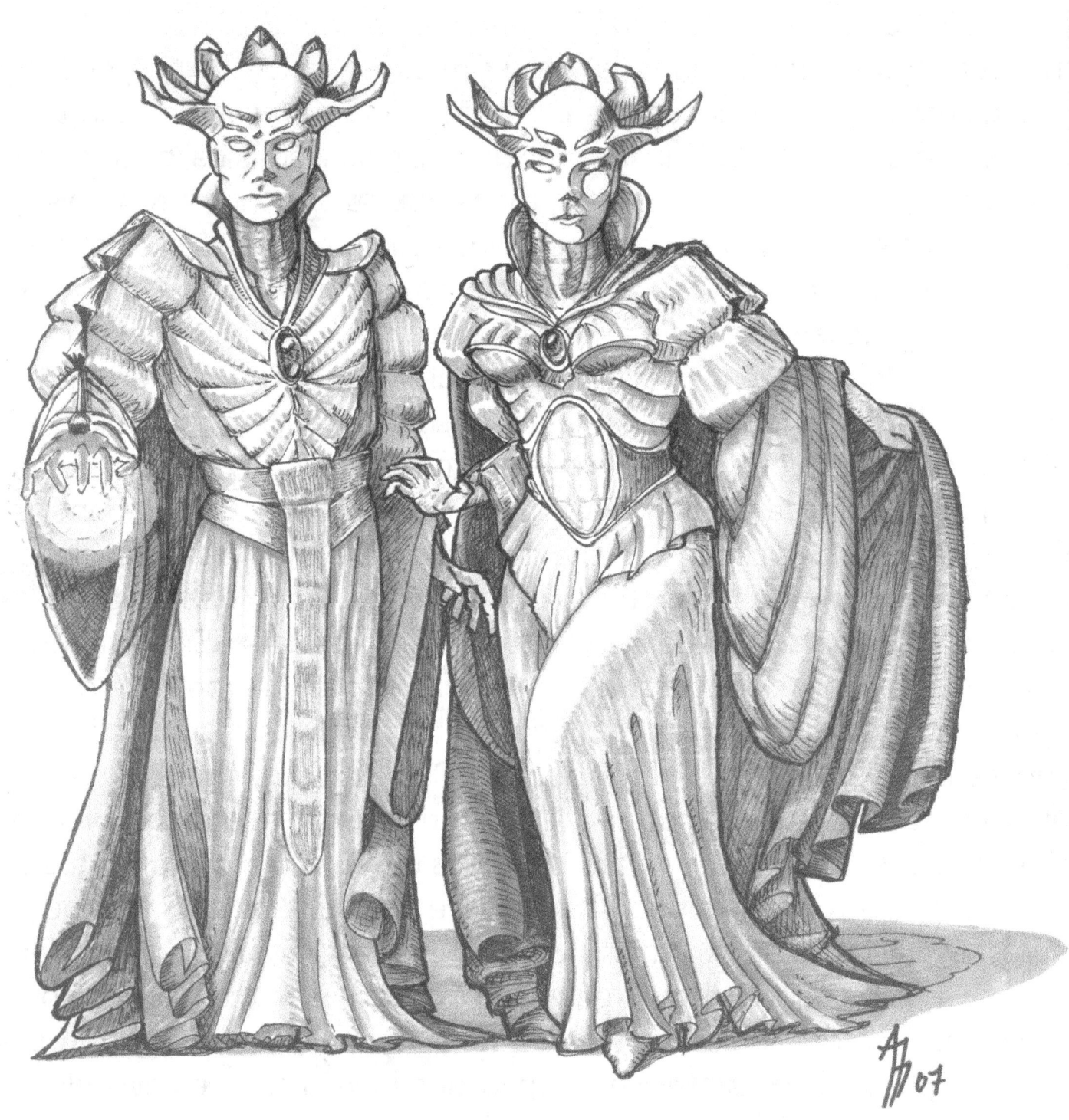

Sovaari Prophets

Species Report - Sovaari
Home Sector - Triumvirate Space
Homeworld - Sovaara (Coordinates 19.10.4-)
Planets in System - 12
Habitable Planets - 10
Planets Inhabited - 9
Planetary Gravity - 3 (Standard)
Dominant Climate - Temperate
Technological Level - 5 (Energetic/biomechanical)
Governmental Structure - Council (Grand Chamber of Insight)
Societal Norm - Tradition
Cultural Emphasis - Knowledge
Miscellaneous Traits - Oldest known race
Lifespan - 1000 years
Physical Attributes - 2.1m height; 210 pounds; Cranial ridge; pale white/yellowish skin tones; yellow eyes; consolidated organs; minimal diet; formerly mated reproduction (ceased about a century ago)

Summary - First race to evolve in Galaxy Prime. Seen as godlike by many species. Supposedly preparing themselves for ascension into higher beings of light, energy or some other form. Trying to unify the galaxy against the Mordas threat. Very wise, noble and pacifistic. Much is unknown about their history, technology and physiology. Intolerant of aggression. Seem to have a sense of endless galactic awareness and knowledge. Exude peace, beauty and tranquility.

Their tech is practically invisible, possibly integrated into their bodies. It is sometimes offered to races to jumpstart their research or to give their society a necessary boost. Their cranial ridge begins closed and opens slowly with age and wisdom. It also help to deflect injury, though few are foolish enough to attack a Sovaari. Formed the Triumvirate with the Gilgari and the Zhani. On good terms with most races and sectors. Affirmed enemies of the Runarians and the Kor.

Their vessels are often oddly shaped and primarily biomechanical. Few, if any, remaining mutations or Kinet in their population. Little use for cyberware or bots, though their androids are practically indistinguishable from a living organism. Most armor and weaponry will be energy-based, yet still utilizing biomechanics.

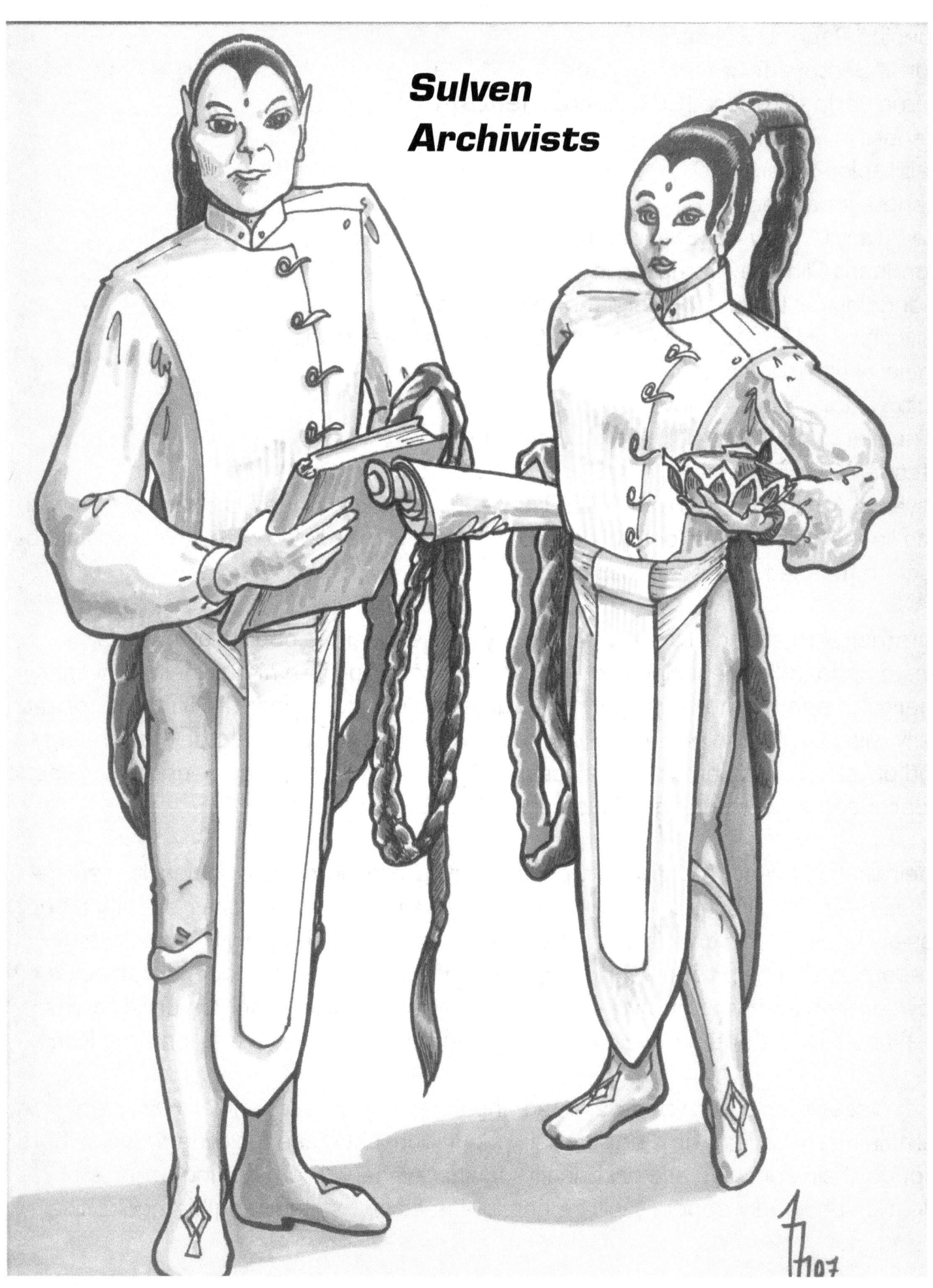

Sulven Archivists

Wisdom of the Sulven

Use the weapons of your enemy and you will soon become an enemy of yourself.

Words of beauty are hollow if they have no meaning.

Beware the helping hand for it may one day become a fist.

Raw strength does not equate with victory.

If you pronounce a man a fool, prepare to find an enemy.

A stone is sometimes just a stone.

Carrying weapons will make you a warrior as much as using a microscope makes you a scientist.

Never let your opponent count to three without a challenge.

Even a virus can be diplomatic, striking all equally without regard for rank or talent.

Regardless of what a leader decides, the people will still implement the decision as they see fit.

The bigger the treasure, the bigger the guardian.

Runarians lie as a matter of course, if only to stay in practice for the really important matters.

There is no practice session for life.

A fool and his credits will soon party.

When in doubt, listen to the man with the higher technology.

Know your enemy as you know yourself and you shall always be victorious.

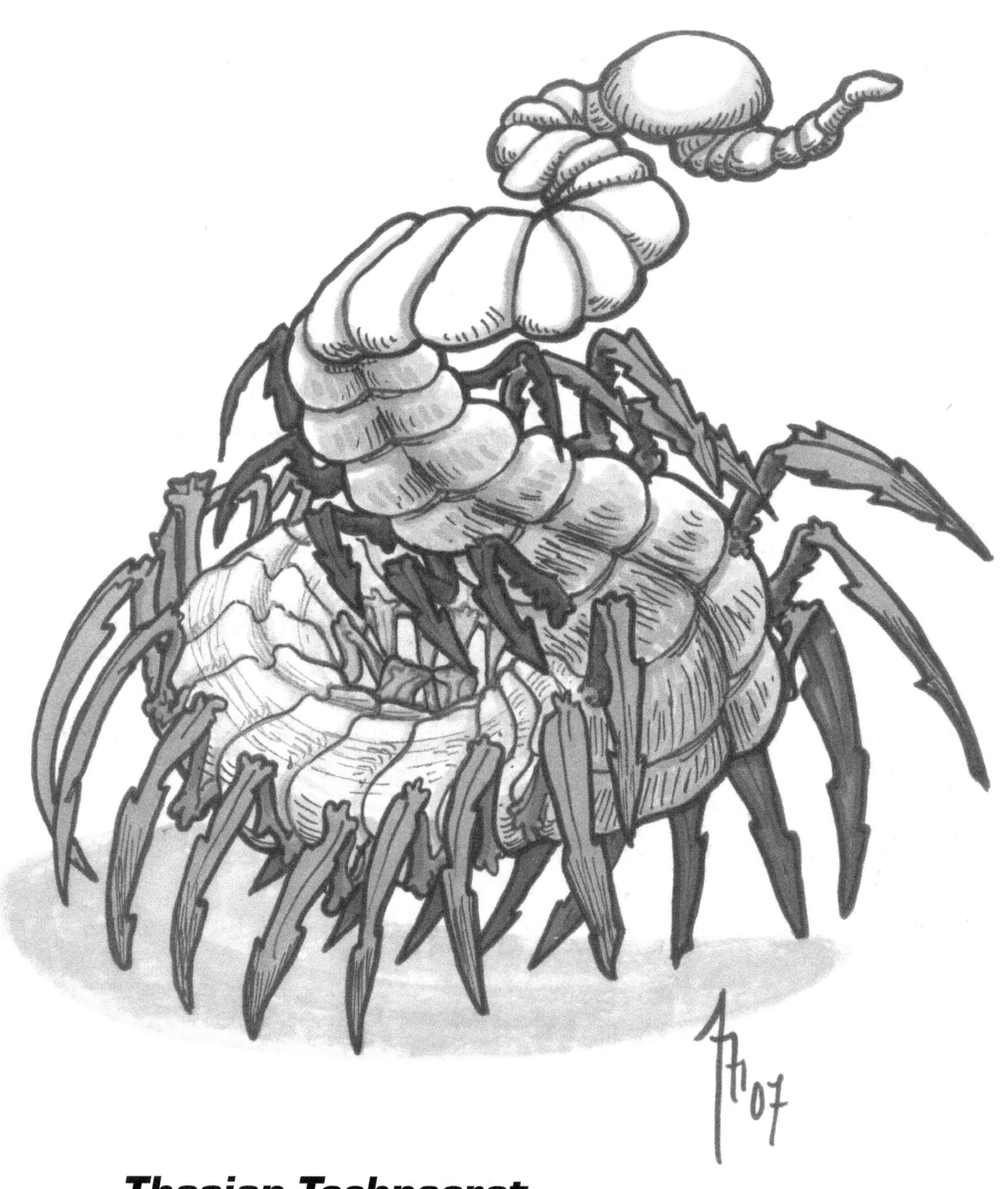

Thasian Technocrat

Expanded Thasian Timeline

2C - Thasians are sole lifeform to crawl out of primordial ooze
4C - Rapid reproduction and migration fills the entire planet with Thasian offspring
5C - Thasian trade and commerce develops quickly
8C - Corporate structure created and cities flourish
1M - Overpopulation threatens society; subterranean and aquatic domiciles built
1M3C - Industrialization creates rapid advances
1M6C - Pollution and waste become a global issue
1M7C - Air travel invented
1M9C - Kor scouting party wiped out
2M1C - Technological age begins based on Kor equipment
2M4C - Scientific advancements solve issues of overpopulation, pollution and waste
2M8C - Worldwide corporate war begins
3M2C - Arrival of Grengi trade fleet ceases internecine conflicts; high tech acquired
3M5C - Governance of Thasia Prime unified under Thatak Corporation
3M8C - Era of space travel begins
4M - Thasia Minor explored and settled
4M2C - Treaties with Taurici empire achieved
4M4C - War with Kunlaati pirates; massive bribes paid to end fighting
4M7C - Thasians invent hypergates; space travel and exploration accelerated; huge financial windfall
5M1C - Envoys sent to far reaches of Galaxy Prime; dozens of treaties negotiated with myriad worlds
5M3C - Thasians reap profits from construction and travel contracts in nearly all sectors
5M6C - Kinet abilities begin to appear in populace
6M2C - Thasians cut off trade with Grengi in favor of Molgans
6M9C - Massive Malborean onslaught wreaks havoc on Thasian worlds
7M1C - Two centuries of reconstruction end
7M4C - Thasian retain services of Riin, Norgh and Izars to guard sector borders
7M8C - Tuth extortion rebuffed; much damage and many casualties reported
8M2C - Sector Marshals formed by Thasian leadership to combat rising crime and piracy
8M6C - Thasians invest in Exomech cyberware; astronomical amounts of currency attained
9M - Thasians claim economic dominance over 2 sectors of space
9M3C - Sector Marshals compete with L'krian Law Syndicate over dispensation of justice
9M7C - Drishix swarms roam out of control on Thasia Prime; many thousands dead from thier stings
10M1C - Thasians buy up colonies, moons and planets from Taurici and others
10M4C - Thasian Autocracy officially recognized

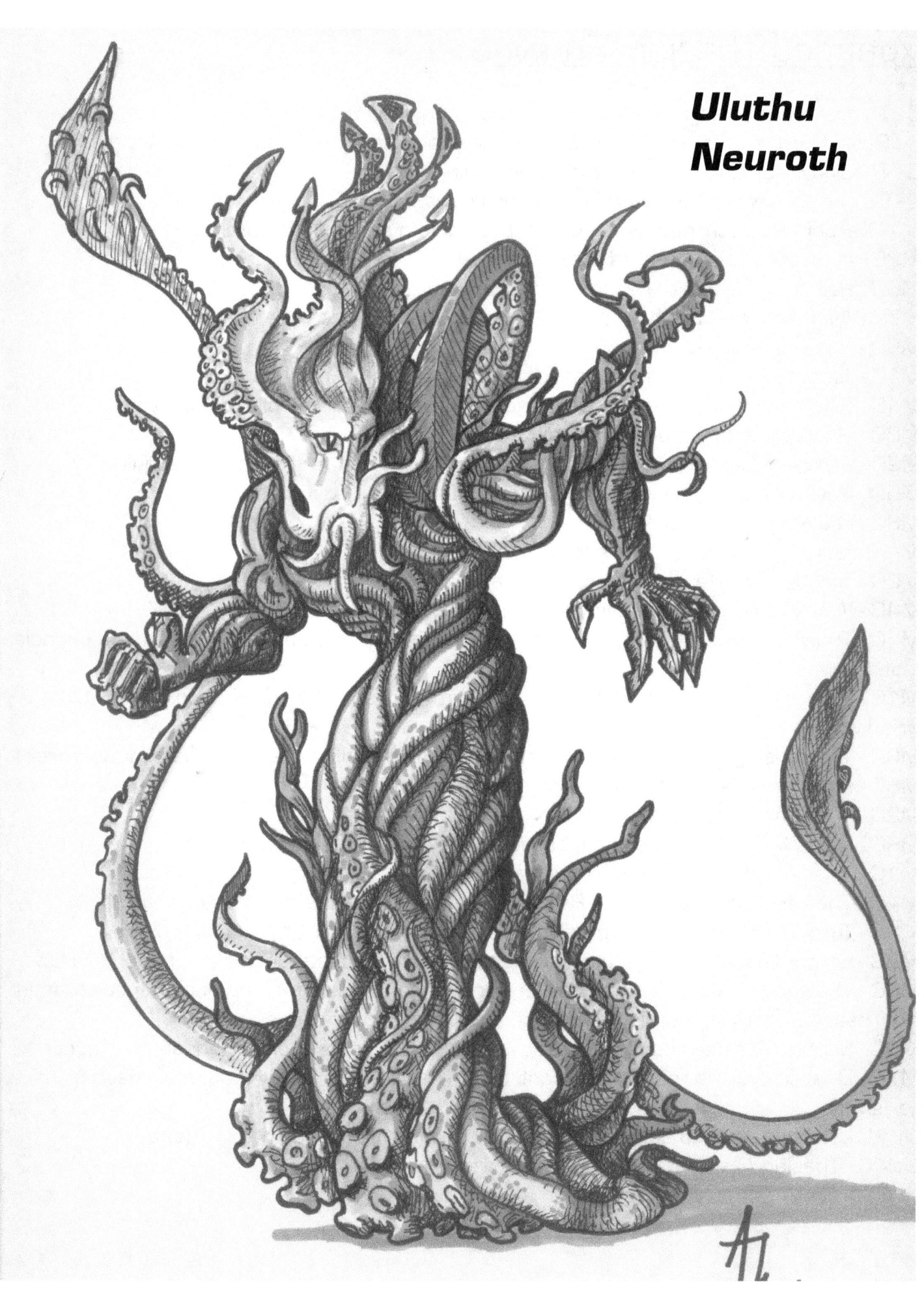

Uluthu Neuroth

Uluthu Decree

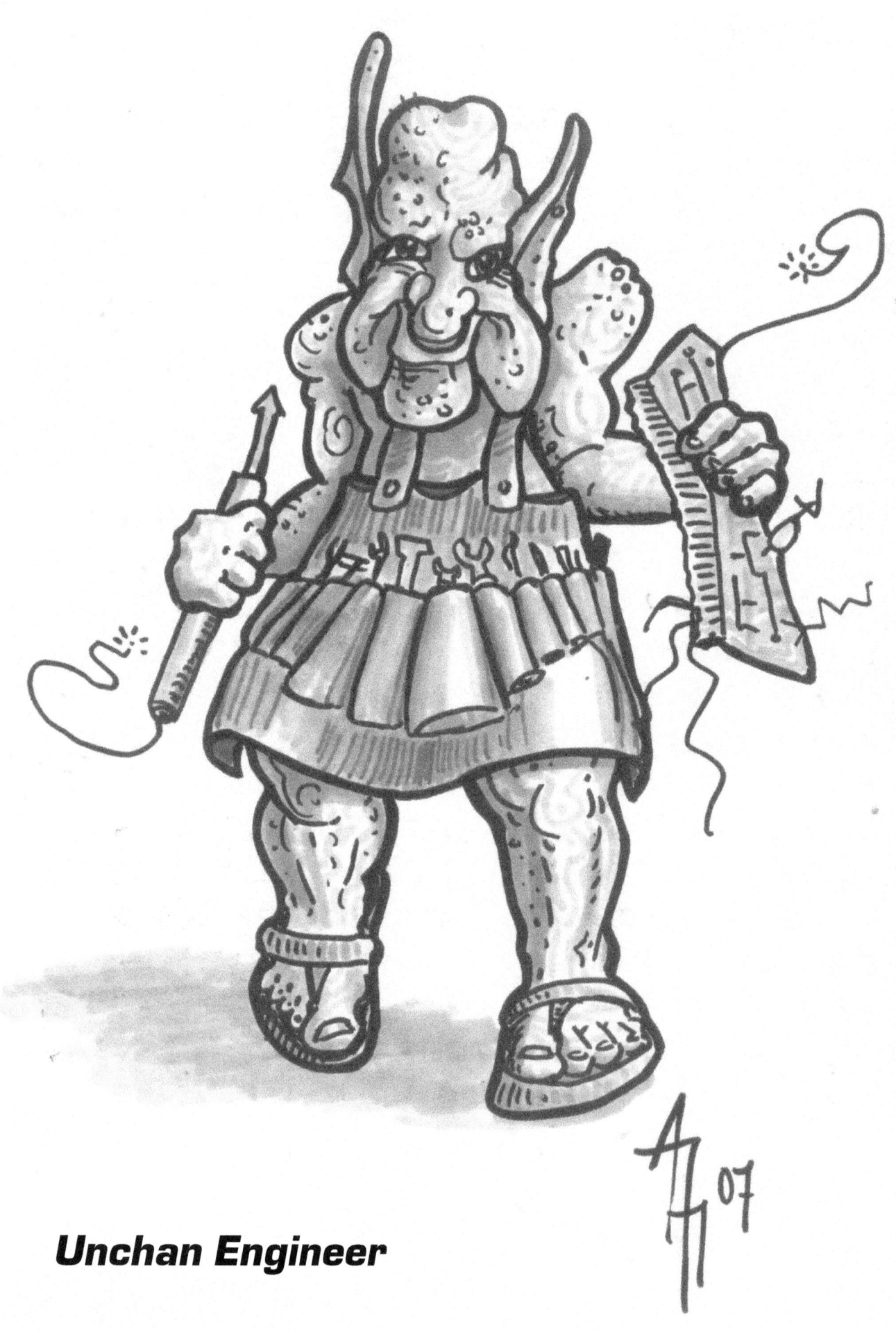

Unchan Engineer

Creator's Commentary on the Uncha

Short and ugly, these little guys are the technical wizards of Galaxy Prime. Maybe that is why they are so valued by just about every race and why the Kor have blockaded their homeworld to make sure that none of them escape. Their name is partially derived from the sound they make when they speak, sort of a piggish, grunting noise. They are a submissive race, though, with no overall plans to escape from under the thumb of the Kor (or anyone else who sees fit to enslave them). As long as they can dabble, tinker and fiddle with things they are fairly content. Surprisingly, even with all of their mechanical aptitude they are still considered to be a Tech 3 industrial culture. Most believe that it won't be long until they reach Tech 4 and really start to dominate the galactic scene. They are extremely organized, having set up their society into a synergistic series of guilds that allow them to have a kind of "conveyor belt" culture that sees much progress in very little time. Yes, they are the ones that can throw together some goose feathers and duct tape and have it turn out to be a formidable weapon! Alternately, they can repair that giant hole in your starship with nothing but a ball of twine in 3.2 seconds flat (or so the story goes). So valued are their skills and talents that some will actually brave the dangers of the Kor Regime (and the ire of the Kor themselves!) to acquire some technical knowledge or doo-dad from the Uncha first-hand.

Maybe it's because of their height or maybe it's because of their less-than-attractive countenance but few players have been mechanically inclined enough to take the Uncha on a test run. Conversely, one of my best and most memorable NPCs was an Uncha named Grot. He had a voice like Droopy the Dog and a personality to match. Little did the players expect the surprise he presented at the end of that campaign! But people shouldn't get hung up on stereotypes either. How about playing a member of the Clergy, trying to reconcile myth and machine? Or maybe a cute little Uncha assassin? Granted, these lil' folks aren't really into violence but if you do encounter them they will likely take you out with a series of ingenious booby traps, snares and other insidious devices of their own invention...

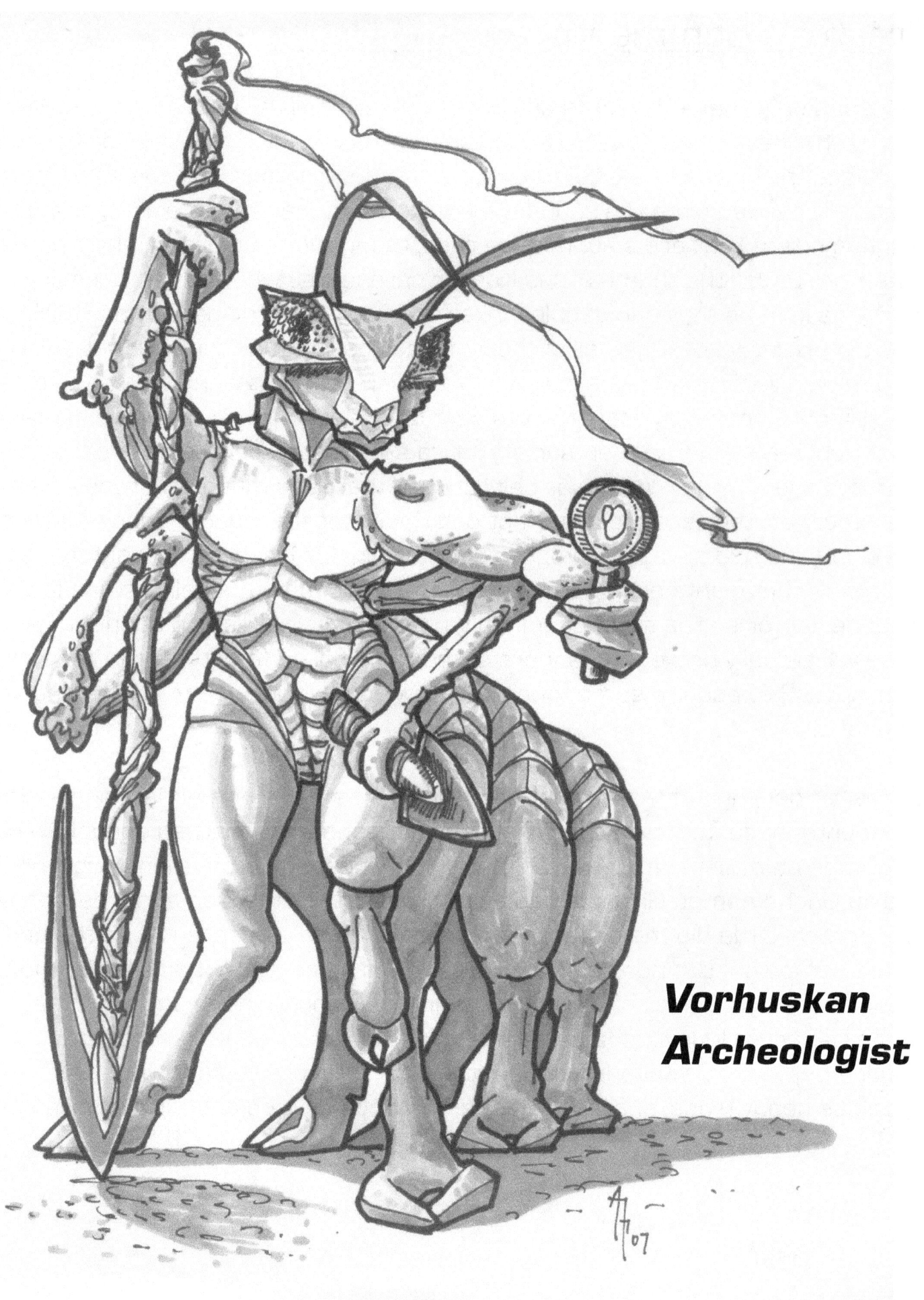

**Vorhuskan
Archeologist**

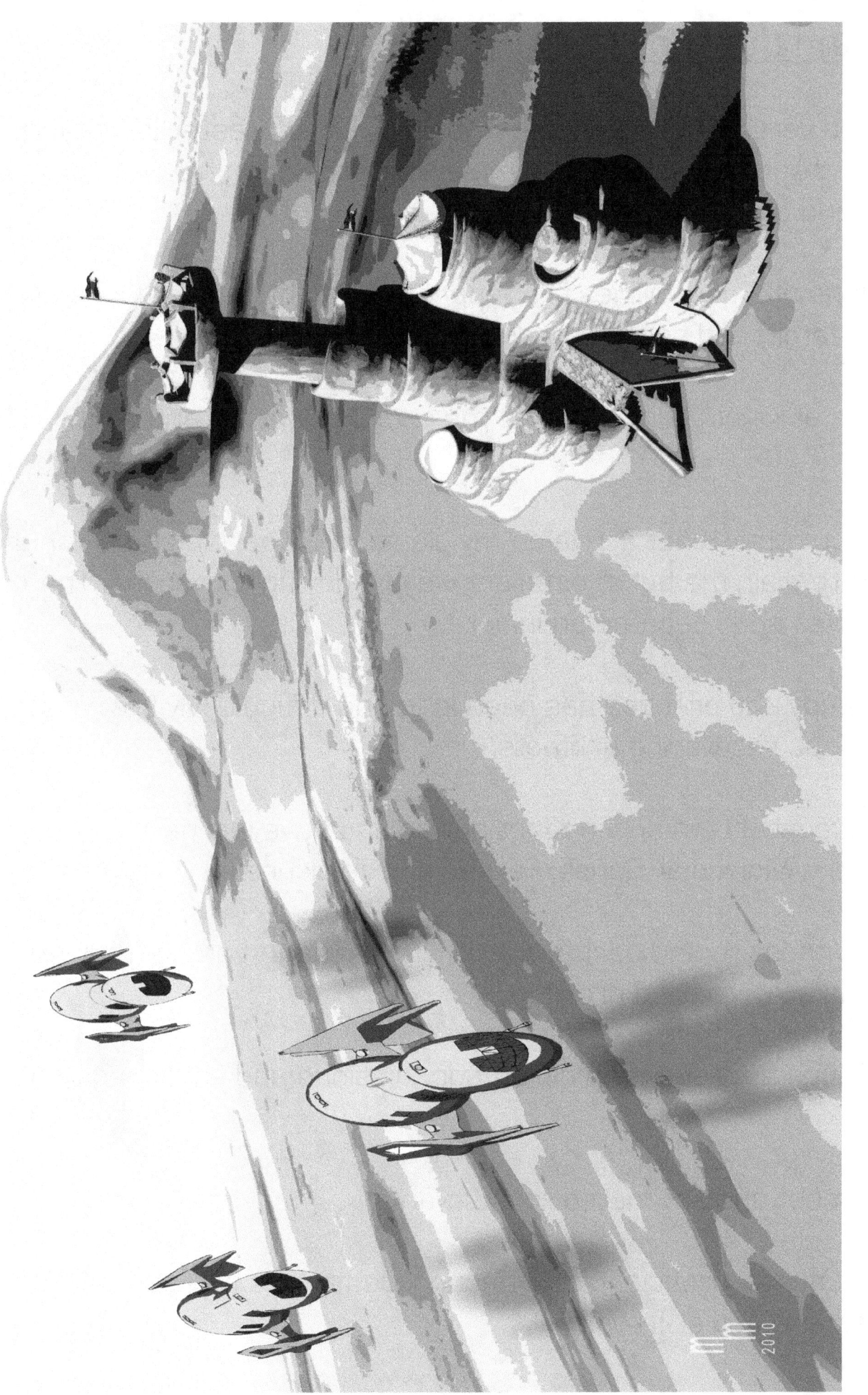

Vorhusk scout ships patrolling the outpost on Nilia-2

Vorhuskan Journal

An abridged version of the journal written by Kinet Master Z'p'tik with excerpts highlighting some of the major milestones on his path of discovery and enlightenment.

Age 5 - Signs of Kinet abilities first appeared. Frightening at first but support of family and society made me to feel special.

Age 7 - Use of Kinet abilities makes me a valued worker and a fun playmate.

Age 10 - Two other Kinet arrive on my planet, a Relgarian and a Yantian. Both offer to train me but in different ways. They fight over me. The Yantian leaves and I become an initiate.

Age 12 - Study and practice has been long and difficult. My first great test is on Tzua recovering artifacts.

Age 13 - Success! I am now a Kinet novice and have learned Psychometry, Molecular Sense, Farsee and Telekinesis.

Age 16 - Witness to and part of the official formation and recognition of the Kinet as an organized group.

Age 18 - Much time spent on diplomatic missions and escorting Arn pilgrims.

Age 21 - I meet and am mated to a Ziryan.

Age 25 - Acquired proficiency in affecting Density, as well as Cosmic Awareness and Astral Travel.

Age 28 - Our ship becomes lost in wormhole. Only my Kinet training saves us. End up stranded in Free Colonies sector. Settle on Omia.

Age 33 - Relgarian Master returns to test me once again. I become an Adept.

Age 37 - Mate passes away.

Age 42 - Bio-cryst manifests itself in my chest. Color is white. I attempt to resurrect mate but fail.

Age 44 - All out war against Tuth as they try to infiltrate Omia and kidnap its natives for experimentation.

Age 46 - Neuroth attempt to convert me. They fail but nearly kill me for refusing.

Age 49 - Relgarian Master dies in battle with Gexran Horror.

Age 51 - Relocate to Frontier Space, hoping for more solitude.

Age 53 - Joranian Kinet arrives to make me full Kinet Master!

(Kinet Master Z'p'tik died peacefully on Planet Zof, never having fully realized his Kinet Manifestation. He was aged 56 years.)

Vosskan Elder

Species Report - Vosskans
Home Sector - Drakasian Annex
Homeworld - Vos (Coordinates 25.6.4-)
Planets in System - 5
Habitable Planets - 3
Inhabited Planets - 2
Planetary Gravity - 4 (Elevated)
Dominant Climate - Swamp
Technological Level - 3 (Industrial)
Governmental Structure - Dictator (Leader: Tyran Terroc)
Societal Norm - Lechery
Cultural Emphasis - Subterfuge
Miscellaneous Info - currently experiencing civil war
Lifespan - 75
Physical Attributes - 3.1 m length; 395 pounds; webbed appendages; dorsal frill; mottled green/brown scales; 2 sets of gills; small sensory whiskers; frequent aquatic egg fertilization (30-40); body requires frequent aquatic submersion; omnivorous

Summary - An aquatic race that can survive for short periods outside of water. They do equally well in fresh, brackish and salt water. Typically slow and lacking in observational acuity. Fierce grapplers with an indomitable will. Though aggressive and combative, they have cultivated the arts of lying, theft, cheating, undermining and betrayal (likely imparted to them by their former Runarian masters).

Their vehicles use simplistic combustion engines but only for land travel as they are full adept at swimming and prefer not to be airborne. They will use hand-to-hand weapons (or simply their razor sharp flippers) in most violent situations. Males and females are equally vicious in their society, regarding all aspects of life, including reproduction.

Transplanted to secondary world by Runarians in order to help the overpopulation issue. Now under yoke of Drakasians. Vosskan society split over which rulers to side with. Some see the Runarians as a more advanced culture and wish to emulate them, while others regard the Drakasians as a more similar lifeform that they can all relate and acclimate to. A fairly dangerous but, as yet, unnotable race that runs the risk of being overshadowed by its evolutionary counterpart, the Eivers.

Tale of the Zhani

Furanji could smell the blood.

In his 16 years of service to the Ocelon faith the clergyman had visited many sites that were the scene of horrific violence and death. And yet he had never smelled this much blood. The heady scent was coming through the air vents and he immediately feared the worst.

"Catja are you smelling what I'm smelling?" asked Furanji through the comm system. He got no response. "Catja can you hear me?"

When his acolyte did not answer, he immediately put the ship on autopilot and dashed into the main corridor. His ears went up, his claws came out and his tail bagan to flick back and forth. Furanji followed the tantalizing odor to the rear of the vessel where the stasis units were kept. There, where the bodies of a dozen dead xenoscientists had been carefully stored, stood a scene of devastation and disgrace. All 12 Inon corpses were badly mangled and shredded, their stasis units destroyed.

A scraping noise made Furanji look to the ceiling and there he saw the perpetrator of this scene in all its awful, unnatural glory: a cypod. Native to the Inon homeworld, these semi-sentient creations were a perfect example of science gone wrong. Part organic, part silicate, they grew, evolved and reproduced by cobbling together bits of electronics, cybernetics and living tissue.

The clergyman leaped without hesitation, certain that this monstrosity had also killed his poor acolyte and friend. The thing moved, surprisingly fast, and Furanji's claws met only unyielding Ileonic bulkhead. The holy man growled in frustration as the cypod dashed into the corridor. He refused to let this creature tear apart his ship!

Furanji gave chase as the thing quickly and easily scaled walls and ceilings, eventually coming to a dead end. The clergyman prepared to pounce and rip the creature apart but it suddenly reversed its direction, springing through the air and landing right on Furanji's face!

The clergyman was momentarily startled and he began to twist and flail wildly. The cypod deployed several needle-like objects, razor-sharp shivs and gnarley exposed wires that still sparked with electricity. Furanji fell to his back and kicked at the thing with his back claws, snagging it and flinging it down the hallway just before it could mangle his face.

But now Furanji had his back to the wall as the cypod renewed its assault. Again it raced towards the clergyman and vaulted at his head with unerring aim.

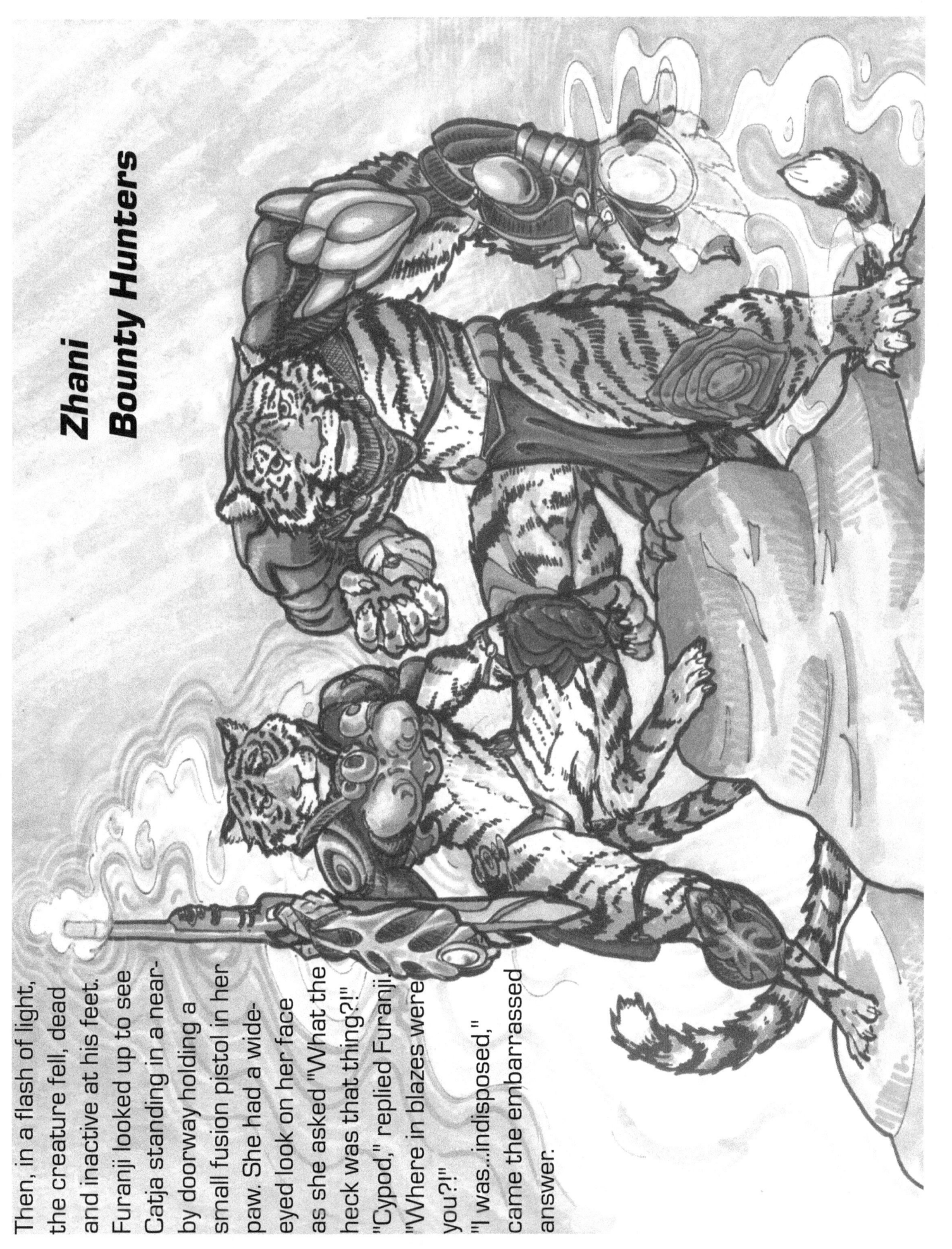

Zhani
Bounty Hunters

Then, in a flash of light, the creature fell, dead and inactive at his feet. Furanji looked up to see Catja standing in a nearby doorway holding a small fusion pistol in her paw. She had a wide-eyed look on her face as she asked "What the heck was that thing?!"

"Cypod," replied Furanji.

"Where in blazes were you?!"

"I was...indisposed," came the embarrassed answer.

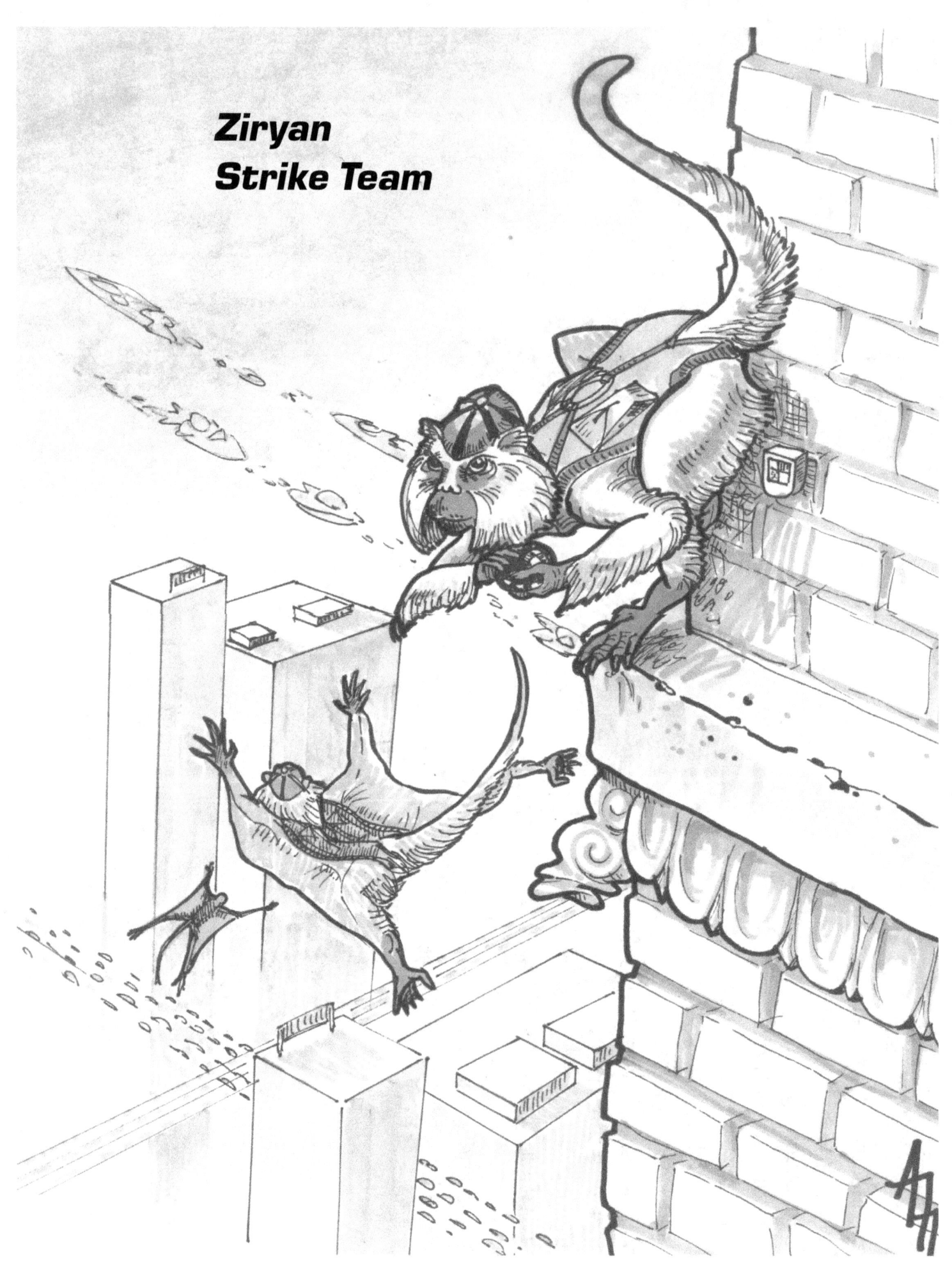

Quoth the Ziryan

If you larn somebody, set them free to jump off a building and float gracefully away.

You cant always steal what you want, but if you try sometimes, you just might find you can convince someone to give it to you for free.

Shooting for thrills is the only way to kill, so I will do your dirty deed for dirt cheap.

Welcome to our concrete jungle, baby. We've got fun, games and a heck of a lot of druzi.

We dont need nothing but a good time and a bunch of credits to spend.

At first I was afraid and petrified until I realized that I would survive...and he wouldn't!

Yes I like to rock. Yes I like to roll. Yes I like to party. I like to do these things all night and every day!

I had 2 tickets to Keramin. I was all packed and ready to leave that night. Then the Mordas came and ruined it all...

I got a new cruiser called the Black Betty. She can ram, she can jam and she can go 5 times the speed of light.

Go ahead! Try and hit me with your best bot!

And the guy in back said to attack so it turned into a cantina crush!

I'd rather have a slow ride and take it easy than have to cram on to one of those faster Nomme transports!

I've never lied and I've always been cool. I wanna be elected to the Galactic Council.

Once my glider membrane heals I'll be flying high again!

One must fight for the right to party with a Nilite!

There is a house in New Zirya they call the Rising Star and its been the ruin of many a poor man and wouldn't you know that I am one?

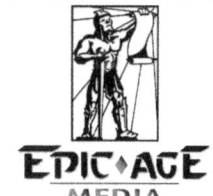

EPIC AGE MEDIA

"The Saga Unfolds..."

ROLEPLAYING GAMES

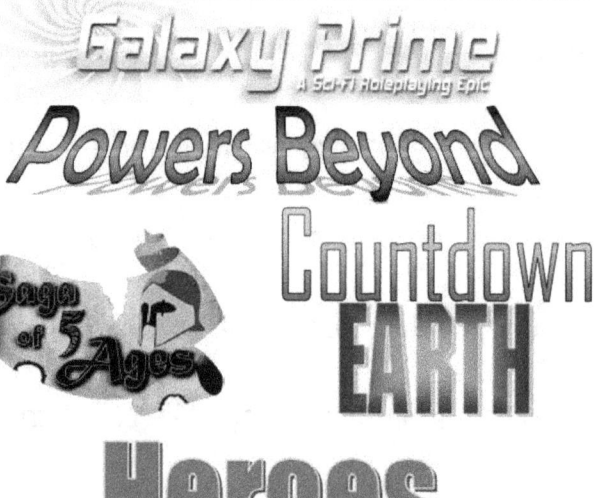

Galaxy Prime
A Sci-Fi Roleplaying Epic

Powers Beyond

Saga of 5 Ages

Countdown
EARTH

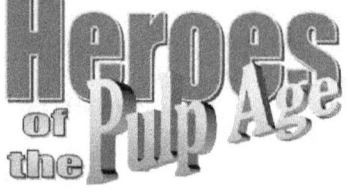

Heroes of the Pulp Age

EARTH THREAT

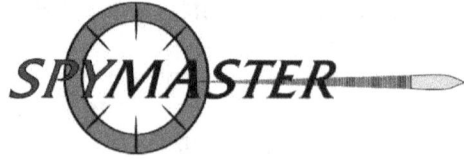

SPYMASTER

BOARD GAMES

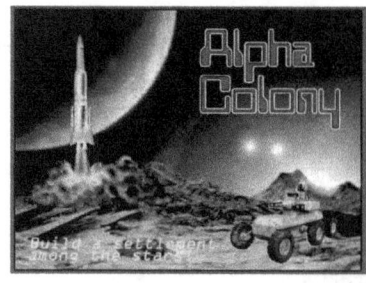

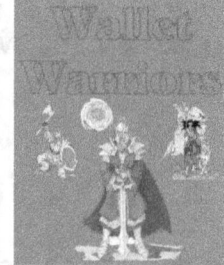

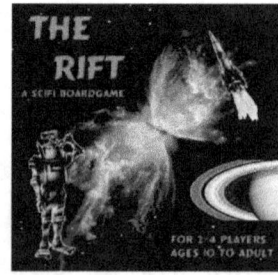

CARD GAMES

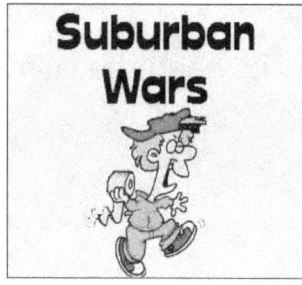

Suburban Wars

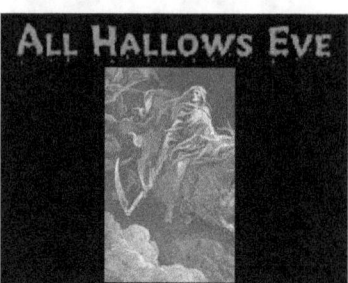

All Hallows Eve

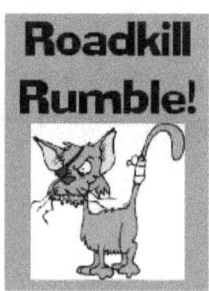

Roadkill Rumble!